City Streets

A Memoir

BY

Frank Del Vecchio

LEAPYEAR
PRESS

For Marian, Richard and Angela

Contents

"The anger is universal when the powerless are overwhelmed by the powerful, especially when the government they hope will protect them is an instrument of harm."

Chapter I

Hot Cat Pilot

"O.K. boys," the Skipper said, "take your plane home for the week-end. See you Monday."

It was a late summer day in 1958. The Skipper was Commander Martin G. O'Neil, Commanding Officer, Fighter Squadron Fourteen, the "Tophatters," the Navy's oldest continuous active duty flight squadron.

Big, ham-handed, a veteran of the brutal air war in the Pacific, O'Neil was the kind of C.O. depicted in the movies. To the two-hundred officers and enlisted men under his command he was a father figure as well as the Skipper. Gruff and detached, as a C.O. has to be, we knew that he was a softy at heart. Our greatest fear was that he would screw up his carrier landings.

Fifteen years after the battles of Tarawa, Saipan, The Marianas, Leyte Gulf, this old tail hook pilot was commanding a bunch of energetic young jet jockeys. We were flying one of the earliest carrier aircraft that could go supersonic — just barely: the McDonnell F3H-2N "Demon." It was heavy and underpowered, but could hit MACH 1.3 in afterburner. It was a bear to land. The cockpit was far forward of the swept wings, and its landing approach was nose high, twenty feet off the deck. You could barely see over the nose. The final approach had to be "dirty": full flaps, speed brakes out, power high in order to retain thrust if you missed a wire, at which point you firewalled the turbine, cleaned up, and went around again, with every eye above deck looking at you.

The skipper may have been a terror as far as the Imperial Japanese Navy was concerned, but when it came to catching a wire on the USS

Franklin D. Roosevelt, CVA-42, the terror was the embarrassment of the C.O. botching his landings.

Minimizing the embarrassment was the task of the squadron Operations Officer, LCDR Francis Murphy. He would schedule the Skipper only for daytime flight operations and calm seas. There was never a wink or a snicker from anyone. Skipper O'Neil had our respect. "Murph" was also ready to give the married pilots a break. They were a little more hesitant to be assigned night bad weather operations than the others: "Dud" Dudzic, Bob Fabiszewski, "Mo" Barnes, Gene Fitzsimmons, Gerry Barente, Bob "Loc" Lynch, Harry Milner, Gene Lund, me. I was eager for those assignments.

My self-image was a fearless street kid. As a Naval Aviator I had found the perfect stage on which to play that role. On the Roosevelt, I volunteered to be the "hot cat" pilot.

The hot cat pilot was the first line of defense for our Fast Carrier Task Force—Carrier Division Two, Sixth Fleet. At night, when most of the crew, exhausted by daytime flight operations, were sacked out below decks, the hot cat pilot was entrusted to protect the carrier and all the ships in the task force. He sat in a fully armed interceptor that was positioned on the steam catapult, plugged in to the auxiliary power unit (APU), all systems activated, ready for the launch order. The instruments were illuminated in a soft red glow that preserved his night vision. The carrier deck was dark and quiet except for the starboard green running light and red to port. The bow spray sometimes churned up luminescent sea creatures.

I was in my element. I wore a red bandana around my neck, ready to perform, to play a role, to show off. That was me — the eager kid in the classroom always shooting up his hand before the teacher even finished asking the question, the youngster wearing a straw hat and twirling a walking stick, singing "The Yellow Rose of Texas" at a Settlement House talent night. Now, the only eyes that were on me were those of the Captain on the bridge, and the flight deck sailors ready to fire up the Demon's Allison J71 turbojet engine.

When Air Control picked up a bogey on its radar — usually a French Mystere or Italian Fiat in a NATO exercise probing the carrier task force's perimeter — the voice of the Air Boss would come through my earphones: "Prepare to launch!" Immediately I would see an illuminated red wand rotating, signaling that the APU was starting the turbine. By the time the carrier had turned into the wind I had checked the engine instruments, cinched tight the seat restraints, pulled down my visor, and was ready for launch. The command came. Up went the blast shields. I pushed the throttle past the detent into afterburner, wrapping my gloved fingers around a small metal post so that my grip would not be loosened by the 3G cat shot. I gave a salute, meaning "Ready"; the green wand went horizontal as the flight deck crew ducked, and the catapult bridle threw the fully loaded twenty ton Demon into the air at about 130 knots, forcing my helmet against the headrest. Immediately when airborne I leaned into the radar hood where the flight instrumentation and the intercept information was displayed. Visual flight over the ocean at night is impossible anyway. Air Control gave me a vector (compass heading) and "Angels" (altitude) to aim for, and the intercept was underway.

VF-14 was the only all-weather night fighter squadron in the task force. If it were combat the other aircraft in the squadron would be launched. But on these NATO probes it was only the hot cat pilot — me much of the time.

We offered a big surprise on our intercepts. We were the first Navy squadron to be equipped with the Sparrow III air-to-air semi-active radar guided missile. It enabled us to accomplish what fighter pilots before us could never do in aerial combat — engage an opponent head on while he was approaching, even from a point a few thousand feet below the attacking aircraft.

The classic dogfight maneuver was to get on the opposing fighter's tail or pull to the inside of his turn so that your guns were aimed at a point just ahead of him — a lead — for a burst. The introduction of the Sidewinder heat-seeking missile, which we also carried, simplified the intercept solution, for it could acquire, (find and lock onto), a jet's hot exhaust from a cone behind. This was more effective against slower-moving jet bombers than high performance fighters.

The Sparrow's head-on capability changed the game forever. This gave me a chance to show off again, beginning with the air controllers who were unfamiliar with what we could do, trying to position me for a tail intercept. I would reply "Negative," then astonish them by requesting a vector for a head-on attack. Later, this young lieutenant would be given the assignment to go from ship to ship to brief the controllers and the brass on the new Naval warfare: the ships could be dispersed in a greater radius from the carriers than before because the interceptors could carry out head-on Sparrow III intercepts. I was lecturing the Admirals!

On this warm Florida day, Fighter Squadron Fourteen Commanding Officer Martin G. O'Neil was telling his young pilots they could take a squadron Demon home for the weekend. Our home station was Cecil Field, Jacksonville, Florida. Home for me was Boston's West End, a thousand miles away. I put my Navy blue dress uniform into a single-suiter, packed a couple of white shirts, a ditty bag and spit-shined black shoes, checked the upper air winds in Aerology, and filed a flight plan direct from NZC Cecil Field to the South Weymouth Naval Air Station, NZW. That would be a stretch for the Demon, but I was counting on the jet stream to whisk me along. What happened when I got to Boston forever changed me.

Stretching the Flight

I entered the airspace controlled by the New York Air Traffic Control Center at a cruising altitude of 39,000 feet with my fuel gauge reading under 1500 pounds, far less than SOP required. But at this point I was committed to making it nonstop to Naval Air Station South Weymouth. A less ambitious plan would have been to refuel halfway, at the Oceana, Virginia, Naval Air Station. But I was eager to get home. I was a single seat jet fighter pilot, alone and totally self-confident. Besides, a buddy was going to pick me up at the field.

When I was handed off to the Boston Air Traffic Control Center I requested a straight-in approach to runway 35, South Weymouth. I throttled back into a long, silent, 150-mile glide, one eye on the fuel gauge, the other looking for the field's landmark nineteen-story high blimp hangar. I was down to 800 pounds of fuel, way low, when I saw that reassuring sight. The only aircraft in the landing pattern, I kissed down with a short rollout because the plane was so light. The ground crew directed me to a tie-down spot and chocked the wheels. I unstrapped, perched my helmet on the joystick, climbed down the precarious footholds from the cockpit to the wing, picked up my overnight bag, and went into the hangar to fill out the post flight log.

My Demon aroused curiosity. It was the first one they had seen at the field. South Weymouth was a quiet air station that had been a World War II base for antisubmarine warfare blimps. It still housed a few blimps and multiengine ASW prop aircraft. (My best friend, Rick Breitenfeld, who chose the blimp pipeline after basic flight training, told me that when they had an emergency they would pour a cup of coffee and discuss what to do.) I was playing the role of the cool Demon Driver, a VF-14 Tophatter. I changed into my dress blues, two gold Lieutenant stripes on each sleeve and aviator wings pinned above the chest pocket, wearing my officer's cap with a white summer cover and the gold navy eagle & anchor emblem.

My buddy picked me up in a blue & white Buick Century convertible. We merited a snappy salute from the Marine at the gate, and then were on the road for Boston. This was the beginning of a perfect day.

Mamma Mia

We head for the small house in South Medford which my parents moved into from the West End. There, we are certain to be greeted with an ear-splitting scream of delight from my mother and a kitchen table full of food. My father, Frank, Sr., will wait until we're seated, unable to escape, to launch into his joke routine, laughing uproariously as he tells them. Everyone has heard these jokes a million times, but they can't help laughing, for my father's manic delight in his own story-telling is infectious. Everyone laughs with him no matter what the joke is and how many times he tells it.

There was the old Jew who asked the doctor if he could change his ethnicity because he had been Jewish long enough. After examining him, the doctor says he could perform an operation which would make him Polish, but there was a catch. Half his brain would have to be removed. After a pause, the old Jew says "O.K. I've been Jewish all my life; I'm ready to try something else." The operation was performed in an operating amphitheatre packed with medical students. The patient awoke from the anesthesia to see a very concerned doctor peering down at him. The doctor says: "Thank God, you survived. But I have to tell you something. We had a complication and had to remove your *entire* brain." After a pause, the patient exclaims "Mamma Mia!" My father slaps his palm to his forehead as he delivers this punch line. His eyes fill with tears of laughter. He slaps his forehead again: "Mamma Mia!" We cannot help but join in the hilarity as we watch this inspired performance.

The old Italian family patriarch is on his deathbed. He announces to his wife and family gathered around that if, after his death, his wife takes up with another man he will dig himself out of the grave and get revenge. He dies. At the burial the wife orders that the casket be lowered upside down. They ask her why. She answers: "Let him dig!" My father, delighted with himself, laughs so hard he loses his breath. The joke is not funny, but his performance is.

"How do you make a squash pie?"

"I don't know, how do you?"

"Sit on it."

He laughs. He is delighted with himself. This does not even qualify as a joke but he makes you feel good. My mother puts food on your plate. She opens and closes the oven door checking on its contents and brings out breaded veal cutlets and "coteca braccioli" — pigskins rolled up with raisins, red peppers, olive oil and spices. We eat in the kitchen. We live in the kitchen. My parents work in the kitchen, assembling the toys and novelties my father, a balloon peddler — "Frank the Balloon Man" — sells on the streets of Boston.

Chapter 2

Roofs, Cellars, Alleys

Violin Lessons

The route home took us along the Charles River by the Hatch Memorial Shell. Every summer members of the Boston Symphony Orchestra, Arthur Fiedler conducting, performed free classical concerts on its stage.

The Hatch Shell was located in the Esplanade, a green ribbon of parks created by Boston Brahmins. Those parks served as a legacy for the city's Irish, Jewish and Italian immigrants. I was a beneficiary. I grew up in the adjacent densely populated West End neighborhood. The Esplanade was my back yard.

There were no trees or grass along the streets of the West End. In summer, my mother would take me to the Esplanade to escape the heat radiating from the pavement and the brick tenements. She would sit on a bench reading while my father picked dandelions and I explored. The Esplanade became my territory. Street kids learn their territory. I knew the best spots to drop a fishing line and catch carp, hornpout, shiners, perch and eels. I knew where to crouch to watch couples kissing in the bushes.

We lived in a twelve dollar a month three room cold water flat at 21 Eaton Street. My father worked pick and shovel as a laborer and my mother was the admitting nurse's assistant in the Outpatient Clinic of the Massachusetts General Hospital. On her way to work she entrusted me to Officer McCarthy, who made sure I safely crossed Cambridge Street on my way to the Sunnyside Day Nursery on Hancock Street, Beacon Hill.

The nursery school was another Brahmin legacy from which I benefited. Miss Gould, a very severe Beacon Hill lady, ordered the children to brush their teeth with salt and swallow an obligatory spoonful of cod liver oil. Lunch consisted of boiled cabbage, squash, and liver which made me gag. The ladies were nice but they couldn't cook. We took a midday nap on wood-slat platforms that folded out from the walls. I found out what was necessary to be considered a good boy. I learned to spell, read, recite and be polite. I became a favorite, but lost that status when I caused Lloyd Brodt to break his leg. We were learning to roller skate. I was intent on winning an imaginary race. I bumped into him. He fell and broke his leg. The ladies were concerned about him. Lloyd Brodt became the favorite. I became his enemy.

In 1938, age five, I entered the first grade at the Peter Faneuil School on Joy Street, Beacon Hill. Miss O'Meara was the teacher. Second grade was Miss Silverman, third Miss Calnan, and fourth Miss Sullivan.

One day Miss Sullivan announced that the Boston School Department was offering free drum or violin lessons, but the students would have to buy their own instruments. The cost of drum pads and drumsticks was two dollars; a violin ten. When she asked who wanted to take drum lessons Amelio DeFranco and Joe Maccarone raised their hands. When she asked who wanted to take violin lessons up went the hands of Asher Neyhus and Henry Metzger. They were the smart kids in the class. I raised mine.

I asked my parents if I could take violin lessons. A violin would cost ten dollars. My mother's pay was ten dollars a week for working Monday through Friday, and Saturday morning. My father, who had been promoted from laborer to timekeeper on a WPA project, made thirteen dollars a week. They said yes.

Stacia Romanoff gave violin lessons in her Phillips Street apartment on Beacon Hill.

An upright piano stood against the wall alongside bookcases and paintings, in a room darkened by drapes that muffled street noise. The violin case on a table in the center held a red violin, a pitch pipe, a stick of rosin, and the bow.

My first task was to tune the violin. As Miss Romanoff tapped out a note on the piano keyboard I turned the tuning peg for each of the strings: E, A, D, G, and plucked the string until its pitch matched the note being played.

Next was use of the bow. I roughened the horsehair with rosin which makes the violin strings vibrate as the bow is drawn over them. I stood next to the piano, held the violin in my left hand, placed my chin on the chinrest, and drew the bow over the strings by moving my right forearm back and forth as instructed. This produced nothing but screeches as the bow bounced and slid from one string to another. I spent the rest of the time trying to get the bow under control.

Miss Romanoff finally called an end to this display and directed me to sit on the couch. She took her own violin out of a brown cloth-covered violin case with a red velvet interior, and played.

Each week I had a lesson. I soon was able to control the bow so that it didn't bounce or screech, played scales, and learned simple compositions.

I drew notice when I walked through the streets of the West End carrying my violin case. Ladies smiled at me. Men, who ordinarily ignored young boys, gave the case and me a glance. Older boys sized me up. I was vulnerable. I knew, however, to make eye contact — a signal that you are prepared to fight — and was able to pass without incident.

I proved a disappointment to Miss Romanoff. Although I practiced an hour a day, it was clear that I would not become a virtuoso. My parents, on the other hand, were very pleased. I could play recognizable melodies, which delighted them.

The major benefit I received from my violin lessons with Stacia Romanoff the winter of 1941 was being introduced to classical music.

When the summer arrived, the concerts at the Hatch Shell became my destination.

Frank the Balloon Man

My father, Frank, Sr., rented a small storefront opposite our Eaton Street flat, where he stored the balloons and novelties he peddled on weekends and holidays. Each day, after returning from his WPA job, he would get busy in the store assembling his wares.

Street peddling was a cutthroat business. A peddler, appearing all smiles for the children and courteous towards the parents, would explode if a competitor encroached on the spot of sidewalk he had staked out. Most of the Boston peddlers were Italians, many of them members of extended immigrant families from the same region of Italy. These paisanos would sometimes work the same parade or Italian fiesta. If you took on one of them they would gang up on you. My father always lectured me to "fight for your rights, but use your brains first." He had to figure out how to gain an advantage over a superior force.

He did not have a high regard for the intelligence of his competitors, whom he considered only slightly less ignorant than the Irish cops who pushed them around expecting a payoff. He applied himself to creating products that would attract the customers to him.

One contrivance was a device that stamped eyelets into construction paper cut in a pattern that formed a pinwheel when assembled on an armature. A long brad was inserted through the eyelets, tapped into a dowel, and it was a toy.

An inspired creation was his "balloon man" balloon:

Peddlers inflated a rubber balloon with lung power, knotted the neck of the balloon around the tip of a flexible reed dowel and thrust it into a child's hand. This quick maneuver would force the father to pay, for the child would scream if told to hand the balloon back to the peddler. To draw attention to *his* balloons, my father conceived of a "balloon man" balloon. From stiff cardboard he fabricated a cutout of shoes imprinted with laces. When the knotted neck of an inflated balloon was inserted into a hole in the "shoes," the balloon could be tossed in the air and land on its feet.

It was World War II. Rubber was war material and balloons could not be found. Frank, Sr. located a cheap source for latex medical glove rejects. The result was a "balloon man" balloon invention unique in the balloon peddler universe.

When the glove was inflated the palm expanded into a balloon shape with the thumb and fingers protruding. The fingers were the "hair," the thumb the "nose." Colored documentary seals pasted on either side of the "nose" became the eyes. The knotted cuff was inserted in the hole of the cardboard cutout shoes. This "balloon man," when tossed into the air, would somersault and land on its feet. If not windy, several "balloon men" could be lined up on the sidewalk. Children attracted to this display bypassed the other peddlers, who soon resented my father.

MY FATHER IMPROVED on the "badge board." The badge board was a frame covered with black felt on which novelty buttons were pinned: "*Erin go Bragh*" (for Saint Patrick's Day parades), "*Say You Will Be Mine*," "*Kilroy Was Here*," "*Dirty Rats*" — a drawing of Hitler, Tojo, and Mussolini heads on rats' bodies. The frame could be propped up like a tripod, or carried to work a parade line. This required the peddler to walk briskly along the gutter, making sales to the crowds behind the rope barrier while hustling to keep ahead of the cops intent on getting him out of the way.

Frank, Sr., constantly on the lookout for "something new," would visit Daddy & Jack's Joke Shop for ideas. He transformed his badge board into a portable toy store. To the "Erin go Bragh" buttons he attached green ribbon, a clay leprechaun's pipe, and a lucky four-leaf clover; from "Say You Will Be Mine" hung heart-shaped lockets; from "Kilroy," a small flashlight on a keychain; from the Axis dictators, a knife in a sheath. He composed sayings and imprinted them on large buttons: "*I Love My Wife But Oh You Kid!*," "*NOV SHMOZ KA POP?*" (The latter, an untranslatable question posed by a bearded hitchhiker in a screwball comic strip, became my father's favorite response to an absurd situation.) My father and his friends Boris Mirski and Henry Mazer would sit around the kitchen table composing sayings to print on the buttons. The more ridiculous the lines the harder they laughed. My father was a little asthmatic, which caused him to gasp for breath from laughing so hard, only perpetuating the jollity. Their wives, Aida Mirski, Esther Mazer, and my mother Adeline, would observe these happy, playful little boys, with smiles.

Teens now crowded around my father's badge board. His novelty items were a hit. He had expanded the market beyond toys and balloons for little kids. The competing peddlers would glower, and smoke cigarettes. My father could position himself a distance away, at a location no one wanted, and attract customers. Eventually the other peddlers changed their tactics. Instead of glowering, they became friendly with him. They were out to learn where he got his goods. Soon their badge boards were hung with novelty buttons and leprechauns' pipes. But my father was a step ahead of them.

The peddlers had the wrong instincts and no vision. They were out to make the sale. If a child came back with a broken toy they would blame it on the kid. My father would replace it, sympathetic that the toy didn't work. This paid off in goodwill. Although peddlers didn't have a fixed location, a store, a landmark, they returned to the same events each year: Saint Patrick's Day (Evacuation Day) Parade, Patriot's Day Parade, Memorial Day Parade, Bunker Hill Day Parade, Fourth of July Parade, Labor Day Parade, Columbus Day Parade, Armistice Day Parade. My father developed a reputation. Parents would go looking for him on these occasions. He was "Frank the Balloon Man."

Eventually, it dawned on the other peddlers that what they had been doing was stupid. They now replaced a toy that was broken and even a balloon that popped. Notwithstanding, this did not prove enough to lure customers away from my father. He had something the others couldn't learn — a humorous attitude toward life, and kindness.

FRANK DEL VECCHIO

Sweet Adeline

"Sweet Adeline,
My Adeline,
At night, dear heart
For you I pine
In all my dreams
Your fair face beams
You're the flower of my heart,
Sweet Adeline."[1]

WHEN A PATIENT walked into the Outpatient Clinic of the Massachusetts General Hospital, he was greeted by Adeline Giacoppi. MGH had been founded to serve the poor; the rich were cared for in their homes. In 1923, its patients were poor Irish, immigrant Jews and Italians.

Every day, sun, rain or snow, a waiting line of people stretched a hundred feet along Fruit Street under a protective overhang. As a person entered, Adeline, dressed in a hospital uniform that most thought was that of a nurse, asked questions, then handed the patient a colored slip of paper. She told the patient to follow the line of the same color painted on the floor that led to the right examining room.

Adeline lived only a block away on North Anderson Street in the West End. She had accompanied relatives to the clinic and helped them communicate with Miss Campbell, the admitting nurse. Miss Campbell asked her to work at the hospital helping with admissions.

Adeline loved the attention the job gave her. She was accepted by the Irish nurses because she was efficient. She could communicate in Italian and enough Yiddish to understand the patient's complaint. The doctors liked her because she was gregarious.

She grew up in a predominantly Jewish section of the West End. It was furthest from the North End, whose Italian immigrants had spilled

---

1   (1903 ballad, lyricist Richard H. Gerard, composer Henry W. Armstrong)

over to the adjacent section of the West End. On a Jewish holiday, she was one of only three girls in the classroom. Her family was Italian, her friends, Jewish.

Giuseppe Giacoppi had been a customs guard in the Guardia di Finanza, Palermo, Sicily. He kept his Beretta pistol, which he showed to his grandchildren. His wife, Arcangela, was a member of the Lariccia family from Bari, Apulia, in Italy's boot. Giuseppe peddled bananas ripened in his basement from a pushcart he wheeled around Boston streets. Arcangela rolled cigars at the J.A. tobacco factory on Cambridge Street. Adeline was the third of four children, preceded by Sal and her sister, Mary. Brother Frank was the youngest. Giuseppe never learned to speak English. Arcangela learned it at the cigar factory.

One day a short, fat, Italian immigrant, Frank Del Vecchio, waited in the line outside the Outpatient Department. When he entered, Adeline Giacoppi directed him to follow the colored line to the examination room. He returned the next day and she gave him the same instructions. The following day he was there again. Adeline asked him why he had to come back each day to see the doctor. Frank said he wasn't coming back to see the doctor, he was coming back to see her.

This process was repeated and became a routine. Adeline gave him no encouragement, but he did not give up. Frank began composing letters to Adeline, which he would drop off at the hospital before taking the streetcar to work. If she was not there he would leave the letters with Miss Campbell. The story about a short, fat, immigrant Italian who was leaving love letters for Adeline Giacoppi spread among the hospital staff, nurses and doctors. Adeline was embarrassed and ignored him. He persisted.

Frank was a self-described "greenhorn" — an unschooled immigrant. He arrived at the Boston docks in 1912, age twelve, from San Sossio Baronia, a small town in Avellino Province. There, his father, Vito, repaired shoes and made leather straps and aprons. His mother, Rosa, tended the animals kept on the ground floor of their house, and was a healer. She had learned how to set animals' broken bones and prepare other remedies such as poultices for injuries and infections.

In the United States, they rented a tiny four-room flat at 110 Prince Street in Boston's "Little Italy" — the North End. There was a common toilet in the hall. No bath. Toilet paper was pages of the newspaper "*La Gazzetta*" cut into squares. The flat was packed with their four children: John, Frank, Lena and Angelo, and three little girls, sisters Ann, Grace and Rosie, whom they took in because their parents couldn't raise them. Vito worked as a laborer. Rosa was a healer. Every Sunday the steps leading up to their flat were filled with men waiting to be healed, carrying bread, sausages, wine, cheese, as payment. Rosa set bones, made poultices, and placed arms in slings. There was always food in the house. Young Frank went to "Greenhorn" school for three years to learn English. He checked out library books and took them up to the attic to read. There was no room in the flat.

Frank's letters to Adeline were slowly written in a careful hand. He included poetry he copied from library books. Adeline did not respond, and eventually Frank stopped leaving his letters at the Outpatient Clinic. She began to have second thoughts. Then, one day, he arrived assisting a patient who needed help. Adeline relented, and said she would see him. In 1928, five years after beginning his courtship, Frank married Adeline in Saint Joseph's Roman Catholic Church on Chambers Street in the West End. It was not until then that he told her the "patient" he was assisting the day she relented was a friend in perfect health whom he had enlisted in his plan.

The Ether Dome

Until the middle of the 19th century, doctors performed surgery with no pain killers for their screaming patients. Speed was essential; quick, bloody amputations the technique. Bloody hands and aprons were the surgeon's trademark.

In September, 1846, William Morton, an inventive Boston dentist, put a patient to sleep with ether gas and pulled out a rotten tooth painlessly. Two weeks after the newspaper account of the painless extraction, doctors at the Massachusetts General Hospital cut a tumor off the neck of a patient anesthetized with ether. The operation was witnessed by an audience of about a hundred doctors and Boston press peering down from seven tightly stacked tiers. Surgery was changed forever. The operating amphitheatre in the hospital's Bulfinch Building became famous as the "Ether Dome."

In 1937, when I was four, nearly every Saturday morning I could be found on a bench in the Ether Dome drawing, or coloring pictures.

Every Saturday my mother took me with her to work at the MGH Outpatient Clinic. The Sunnyside Day Nursery school was closed. At the hospital I was surrounded by caretakers. Nurses and orderlies took me to every corner of the complex. At lab tables I sat on stools and drew. I saw operating instruments being sterilized in metal containers. I watched as carts piled with white sheets were wheeled into a huge, hot, steaming basement laundry complex through one door, washed, dried, folded on long tables, and wheeled out the other end. I rode as a passenger on dollies delivering supplies that were rolled along the underground passageways connecting the buildings. Although I sometimes drew a doctor's quizzical glance, I enjoyed the protection of the hospital workers, and I could explore.

When asked "What do you want to be when you grow up?" I replied, "A doctor." That was the right answer. I could have anything and go anywhere. I could do no wrong.

Roofs, Cellars, Alleys

Jimmy Delmont was a bad boy. He was an Irish kid from a big family that lived across the narrow alleyway from our building on Eaton Street. His father shouted a lot. My father told me Mr. Delmont liked to drink. Sometimes garbage flew out of their window into the alley. My father would wait until Mr. Delmont had slept it off before speaking to him. Mr. Delmont always apologized, said he would clean out the alley and would try his best. After a few days of quiet the scene was repeated.

Jimmy Delmont asked me if I wanted to go exploring with him. I said yes. I was already an explorer. I knew all the underground passageways in the Massachusetts General Hospital, where I could sneak up a dark stairway and crack open a door to peek into a room. It was scary, but if anyone was there I could retreat rapidly into the underground passages where no one could catch me.

The first thing Jimmy taught me about was roofs. He knew buildings that had missing padlocks on the door to the roof. First, we had to get up to the roof. If there were kids on the steps, they would block you if you didn't belong. On the stairway, if someone came out of a flat, we had to beat it downstairs. If anyone was on the roof hanging out laundry we would crouch and sneak by. The tenement buildings were attached, enabling us to go from building to building for an entire block. We ran to the parapet at the side of one roof, sat on it and swung our legs over to the next roof. The problem was when one roof was not level with the next one. The jump down took courage. On the return, Jimmy, who was older, boosted me up.

From the edge of the roof we could spy on the street below. If we were in somebody else's territory and were spotted we had to return rapidly over the roofs to our entry point to escape.

The best thing about exploring on the roofs was looking in windows. We could do this on buildings that were L-shaped at the back or had openings that brought light and air to the apartments. In summer, windows were open, shades up and curtains back. We could see in. If the person inside looked up we were in trouble and had to retreat.

It was too cold to go up on roofs in the winter so we explored cellars and alleys. Alleys were sheltered, cellars were warm. We explored roofs because of what you could see; cellars because of what you couldn't see. They were dark and scary. Alleys piled high with snow muffled your movements; you could spy on people without being detected.

Soon, we tired of exploring cellars and alleys. We spent winters indoors unless it snowed, when we would go to the schoolyard at the end of the street — (Blackstone Junior High School, "the Blackie") — and have snowball fights.

CHAPTER 3

ORIGINAL SIN

At age seven I began preparing for my First Holy Communion. Every Sunday morning after 9 o'clock mass the nuns marched us across McLean Street for Sunday School Catechism lessons. Father Powers took a particular interest in me and became a regular visitor to my classroom. This made me uncomfortable. When he asked my parents if they would permit me to be an altar boy I did not react with the animation I usually displayed when the focus of attention. They told him they would have to let him know. This was unusual. Catholic parents invariably are flattered by an invitation of this kind. I did not become an altar boy. Father Powers stopped visiting my Sunday School classroom.

I applied myself diligently to the Catechism. My mother drilled me until I had every answer memorized:

"Who made the world?"

"God made the world."

"Who is God?"

"God is the creator of heaven and earth and of all things."

I recited the prayers flawlessly.

The Apostles' Creed:

"I believe in God, the Father almighty, creator of heaven and earth, and in Jesus Christ, his only Son, our Lord, who was conceived by the Holy Ghost, born of the Virgin Mary, was crucified, died, and was buried.

"He descended into hell. On the third day he rose again from the dead. He ascended into heaven and is seated at the right hand of God where he judges the living and the dead.

"I believe in the Holy Ghost, the holy Catholic Church, the communion of saints, the forgiveness of sins, the resurrection of the body, and life everlasting.

"Amen."

No matter how hard I tried I did not believe this.

At my First Communion I got a set of rosary beads and was told to pray whenever I was idle. I decided I would say one prayer for every stair we climbed going to Miss Calnan's third grade classroom at the Peter Faneuil School. I reinforced my commitment to the faith by wearing scapulars under my shirt. These were two squares of cloth, each with a holy picture, connected by a chord. One square hung over your heart, the other down your back. The Apostles' Creed, which begins the rosary at the crucifix, was too long to recite on a stair, so I started with the Hail Marys, ten of them, one for each small bead, followed by an Our Father at the fat bead, then ten Hail Marys and one Our Father, repeated until I reached the top stair. It was impossible to actually say the words aloud, so I raced through them mentally as my lips silently moved. I applied myself diligently to this exercise but felt no different at the top of the stairs than I had at the bottom.

During mass I paid close attention to the sequence of movements made by the priest, and was soon able to exactly anticipate when to kneel, stand or sit depending on his progress in the ritual. I could mimic many of the Latin words from memory:

"Kyrie, Eleison — (Lord have mercy on us);

"Christie, Eleison — (Christ have mercy on us);

"Kyrie, Eleison — (Lord have mercy on us)."

In spite of having attended mass their entire lives, most of the faithful didn't know when to stand, sit or make the sign of the cross, and were always late, following someone else's lead.

In order to be in a state of grace for communion at Sunday mass I dutifully made a *good confession* each Saturday afternoon:

"Bless me father for I have sinned. It has been one week since my last confession. These are my sins: I disobeyed my parents three times; I lied four times; I took the name of Our Lord in vain twice."

After this obligatory performance, the priest would wave his hand and mumble absolution in Latin: *"Ego absolvo te a peccatis tuis in nomine Patris, Filii, et Spiritus Sancti."* The penance assigned was always a multiple of Our Fathers and Hail Marys. Thereupon I returned to the pew, knelt, and said the penance, feeling no different after this routine than before.

I SAW MY first Charlie Chaplin movie at the Heath Christian Center Settlement House on a Saturday morning in September, 1942. My exploration of the Massachusetts General Hospital was over; my mother was now at home with my new baby brother, Joey. I was nine, he was six months.

Thirty neighborhood kids waited impatiently for the Reverend Mario Cestaro to set up the projector. The lights went out and a Felix the Cat cartoon came on — a black cat with a white face whose tail was an arrow one minute and a question mark the next. It was for little kids. I didn't like it. Midway through, the film broke and the reel clattered. While Rev. Cestaro spliced the film, the kids held up fingers in front of the beam from the projector to make rabbit ear shadows on the screen. Next was Charlie Chaplin. He frantically tried to keep up with a fast-moving factory assembly line, but the harder he tried the faster it moved. He collapsed at this impossible task and was taken away in an ambulance. After the movie we played games: bean bag, ring toss, pick up sticks, checkers, and put together jigsaw puzzles.

Every Saturday I returned to the Heath Christian Center. Rev. Cestaro organized the boys into clubs that met after the movie: woodworking, photography, drama, chorus, discussion club. Later in the year he removed the benches from the chapel, painted stripes on the floor, attached a basketball backboard at each end, and taught us to shoot baskets.

NEARLY EVERY SATURDAY night in summer the strong voice of a cantor could be heard throughout the neighborhood from the open doors of synagogue Beth Amedresh Agudal Beth Jacob at 31 North Russell Street. I often left the gang gathered around the pinball machine at Charlie Maccarone's store next to the Blackstone schoolyard to see if it was Tabashnik singing. Tabashnik was a frequent presence in the neighborhood. He was powerfully built, bald, with a small beard and a fierce look. His most fearsome attribute was his pace. He would stride furiously down the center of Eaton Street as if pursuing the enemy, stop abruptly, turn, retrace his route, then resume the chase. Sometimes he would stop, calm down, sing in Hebrew to the heavens, then stroll peacefully away. We boys feared Tabashnik, although he never threatened us or did us harm. He never acknowledged us in any way. It was often the voice of Tabashnik I heard during Shabbat services.

At home when I told my mother about these episodes she would nod knowingly and tell me how as a girl she learned Jewish prayers. She would demonstrate this by waving her hands over imaginary candles, then shield her eyes with a hand as she recited:

Barukh atah Adonai, Eloheinu, melekh ha'olam
asher kidishanu b'mitz'votav v'tzivanu
l'had'lik neir shel Shabbat.

I DIDN'T WANT to disappoint my parents about religion so I did my best to please them, especially my mother. It became increasingly difficult for me, however, to accept the doctrines on faith, as required. I sensed my father, as well, was unconvinced, but he never verbalized it. Instead, he applied himself to being useful in the church.

Our parish church, St. Joseph's, was badly run. For example the vigil lights were constantly burning down to the bases, and not replaced. Vigil lights — devotive candles — were an important source of income to the parish, which kept all the proceeds, unlike Sunday mass collections which were split with the Archdiocese.Whenever a Catholic was anxious over the outcome of something over which there was no control it was always a good bet to light a vigil light and ask for Divine assistance. One dropped a dime into the slot at the base of a tier of red or orange-colored glasses holding candles, lit a taper from a candle burning in the tier, and lit a fresh candle. The problem was that the faithful in those Depression years were so constantly anxious that the entire tier of vigil lights would be beautifully glowing with no fresh candles to light. Seeing that the church was losing needed income, my father took it upon himself to replace the burned out candles. When my father told the pastor about the loss of revenue, he saw to it that a storage cabinet was fully stocked with candles and tapers. Because we lived only a block from the church, my father would visit it at least twice a day to replenish burned out candles. He sometimes took me with him, especially during busy Church holy periods, and I soon learned the ropes, going into the vestry for boxes of vigil lights and learning the back stairways between the Upper Church and Lower Church. I explored the back of the church as I had the underground passages at the Massachusetts General Hospital.

Another problem was collecting donations during mass. Wicker baskets attached to long handles were stacked in a corner at the back of the church. At an appointed time in the mass ushers picked up the baskets and took them to the front row, with one usher stationing himself at each end of the row. The basket was passed from person to person down the row. When it reached the end an usher took it and started it back along the next row. Several of the ushers were doddering, not alert, asleep at the switch, failing to hustle the baskets along. Sometimes a basket would get only halfway through the rows when the mass resumed, making collections unmanageable.

Most of the ushers were Irish. The Irish had preceded the Italians into the West End and held the prestigious lay positions in St. Joseph's Church. Without consultation, my father recruited a few of his friends: Gene Gianelli, Freddy Ravenese, Pat Lanciano, and one day according to plan they grabbed the collection baskets, double-timed up the aisles to the front row of benches, and hustled their way through the collection completing it before the ceremony resumed. Though the Irish lay establishment complained, the new breed of ushers received the approbation of the pastor. My father had come up with a better way of doing business for the church, same as he had peddling balloons on the streets of Boston. In our house, the talk about the church was always about how it could operate better, not about faith or souls.

Try as I might I couldn't figure out how to be successful at being a Catholic. I had learned how to be successful at the Sunnyside Day Nursery School. You brushed your teeth, learned your lessons and were polite. At the Peter Faneuil School you obeyed the teacher. At the Massachusetts General Hospital, you spelled big words, like "alopecia areata." But no matter what you did as a Catholic it was never enough. To begin with, even though you had done nothing, you were guilty of Original Sin. Everybody is born with it. Second, you sin if you think bad thoughts. I was constantly thinking bad thoughts. I usually wanted to disobey my parents, I always wanted Lloyd Brodt to get into trouble. "Venial" sins were not really bad and "mortal" sins were very bad, but I didn't have to be told that. I did not believe that a record was being made of all my venial sins and mortal sins and all my thoughts. If I actually *did* something bad, like take some dimes off my parents' bureau, I knew I was doing wrong, but as far as the priest hearing confession was concerned the only difference was the number of Hail Marys and Our Fathers he assigned as penance.

There was no relief if you were a Catholic. Catholics were always guilty. In contrast, the Protestants at the Heath Christian Center did not dwell on sin. They sang hymns and read psalms. My favorite was the 23rd:

The Lord is my shepherd; I shall not want. He maketh me to lie down in green pastures: he leadeth me beside the still waters. He restoreth my soul . . .

Surely goodness and mercy shall follow me all the days of my life: and I will dwell in the house of the Lord for ever.

The Jews moaned and mumbled a lot but always ended with a feast.

Free Speech

There was a commotion from a crowd assembled at the base of the Parkman Bandstand in Boston Common. My father pushed me to the front so that I could see. A man standing on a small wooden box was speaking passionately to an audience gathered in a semicircle in front of him. There was sporadic heckling. When one of the hecklers engaged the speaker in debate, the crowd quieted. As members of the audience drifted away they were replaced by others who had been strolling in the park.

My father said this was free speech which we had in America, one of the things that made this the greatest country in the world. He told me that the Parkman Bandstand was like the "Speakers' Corner" in London's Hyde Park, where a person could advocate unpopular ideas without fear. He told me never to be afraid to speak my mind. He was not afraid to speak his.

One night a few years before, my father returned home red in the face and very excited. He had gone to a meeting of the Ward 3 Social Club, which was run by the Irish political machine that controlled the predominantly Italian North and West End. The speaker was James Michael Curley, "the Silver-Tongued Orator," who was running for a fourth term as mayor against Maurice J. Tobin. When the moderator asked if there were any questions, my father stood up and said, "When is the City of Boston going to pick up the trash and clean up the streets of the neighborhood? Garbage fills the alleys and overfills the garbage cans. The dogs and rats pick at it. It is filthy and unsanitary. The city workers aren't doing their job. They lean on their shovels, smoke, and talk. They got their jobs through political pull and not one of you is worth a damn." Turning to the audience he said: "Come with me and I will show you. Follow me!" As people in the hall began to rise to follow my father, James Michael Curley shouted, "Mr. Del Vecchio is right! I will not let this happen in my administration. I promise you that if I am elected you will see changes in the neighborhood." The crowd calmed. After the meeting some operatives gathered around my father and invited him to a private meeting. At the meeting they flattered him and asked him to support undertaker Joseph Russo for state representative, implying there would be something in it for him. He thanked them and excused himself. He had no use for Russo and other Italians who simply were figureheads for the machine.

My father often told me, "Frankie, the most important thing is education. I was twelve when my family came to America. I didn't go to school in Italy. I went to 'greenhorn school' in the North End for three years and then had to work. There are things I cannot do because I don't have the education, the knowledge to do them. But you can. In this country if you work hard and study hard you can do anything."

My father frequently took me to the Boston Common, usually passing by the Parkman Bandstand, where sometimes two or three debates would be going on simultaneously. If it was a weekday, our route would be up Temple Street, cutting through the State House Annex, then through the Hall of Flags. The Beacon Street exit was dominated by the monumental statue of Civil War General Joseph (Fightin' Joe) Hooker astride his steed.

Opposite the State House, at the entrance to the Common, was an enormous bronze bas relief of marching soldiers: three rows of infantrymen, unmistakably Black, led by a drummer boy and commanded by a mounted officer with saber drawn. This was Colonel Robert Gould Shaw commanding the 54th Massachusetts Volunteer Infantry Regiment of Black soldiers on its doomed Civil War trek to Fort Wagner.

On weekends the State House was closed. Our route then was Tremont Street, where we would stop at the Old Granary Burial Ground, located between Beacon and Park Streets, the burial site of many great men and patriots: John Adams, Paul Revere, John Hancock, Robert Treat Paine, James Otis, Wendell Phillips, Crispus Attucks.

MY FAVORITE SPOT in the Boston Common was the hill in the center, where I could squint through a slit window into the dark interior of a World War I tank immobilized on its concrete base, sit on an artillery piece forever aimed at the Public Garden, or crawl onto an antisubmarine mine perpetually moored there.

One spring day in 1940 my father and I were sitting on that hill, looking out over the expanse below, when he told me apologetically that he had been wrong about Mussolini.

He had often praised Mussolini as a leader who got things done, such as "making the trains run on time," in contrast to the crooked politicians in Boston, who accomplished nothing. He now understood that he, like other Italo-Americans, had been taken in by Mussolini's propaganda. The realization came after listening to two radio commentators he religiously tuned in to: H. V. Kaltenborn and Walter Winchell, who exposed Mussolini's lies and his alignment with Hitler. My father regretted his gullibility and wrote an angry letter to "The Italian News," an English-language newspaper targeting Italians in Boston, for having misled ignorant immigrants. He told me not to accept the words of the powerful, but pay attention instead to what they did.

That summer my father's project was teaching me how to ride the entire Boston Elevated Railway system without paying more than one fare. He learned the system through his job as a WPA project timekeeper. This involved him taking public transit from job site to job site throughout Boston for random checks of attendance. His task was to check the attendance sheets at the beginning of the day, spot check randomly during the day, and check at the end of the day. The timekeeper was unpopular with the workers for obvious reasons — even better than goofing off on a government job in Boston was not being on the job — this was a time-honored political tradition. A city worker would check in for work in the morning, then disappear, and return just in time to check out for the day. The workers had perfected a rotating system where a casual observer would always see a few people at work while the rest went about their merry ways. My father got the job when an area supervisor saw that he came to work in the morning and worked all day until check out time. The timekeeper job was a blessing because he had developed a back problem as a pick and shovel laborer.

Hot summer days were a great time to ride the Boston Elevated Railway system. Air rammed through the latched-open doors that led from car to car of the speeding elevated railway trains and cooled the occupants. Gates prevented passengers from going car to car. The open door of the first car of the train, where the motorman was at the controls, was the ideal spot to stand. As air rushed by we could look far ahead down the elevated tracks and see Boston from a perspective only the motorman and we had.

We began our missions at the Bowdoin Square subway station in the West End. It was the terminus of the East Boston line, which enabled my father to station us so that we were the first to enter the lead car and could position ourselves at the front.

Certain stations in the Boston Elevated Railway system had either pedestrian bridges or underground passageways that enabled a passenger to exit one train and then cross to board a train going in the opposite direction without going through a turnstile. The complex system of transfers, el to trolley to bus, once learned, could be exploited to change from one line to another without having to pay again. My father had mastered the Boston public transit system. It was one of his great accomplishments.

The summer of 1940, at age seven, I learned how to ride all the elevated railway lines, all the subway lines, and all the trolley and trackless trolley lines in the Boston Elevated Railway System, and I saw all of Boston in the process.

Sneak Attack

"Yesterday, December 7th, 1941 — a date which will live in infamy —the United States of America was suddenly and deliberately attacked by naval and air forces of the Empire of Japan."

Franklin Delano Roosevelt, December 8, 1941

I was alone at home when a voice interrupted the Sunday afternoon radio program:

"President Roosevelt said in a statement today that the Japanese have attacked Pearl Harbor from the air."

The next day my father tacked the front page of the Boston Globe to the bathroom door: "Japs Bomb Pearl Harbor." Every day he posted the war headlines.

He was fat, had a bad back, and my mother was pregnant. The Draft Board classified him 4F. He signed up as an Air Raid Warden, and wearing a white armband went around the neighborhood instructing residents to cover their windows with black drapes when the sirens went off. I collected old newspapers and tin cans for the War Effort, which also appropriated the iron fence around the Boston Common. The state legislature ordered the golden dome of the State House to be painted black so that enemy bombers would not find it. People bartered for ration book stamps. Meat stamps were the most valuable. How could an Italian survive without spaghetti sauce?

We now lived at 26 Irving Street in a four-room flat. The Mondellos, Dick and Nellie, were our neighbors. Dick Mondello, who ran a butcher shop on Green Street, received greater deference than the politicians and mafioso. My mother was Nellie's best friend, who lived in mortal fear of him. Dick was an imposing man with a pencil moustache and slicked down hair. He split whole sides of meat with a swing of his cleaver. His white apron was perpetually spattered with dried blood, as was the sawdust-covered floor. He carried a huge roll of bills and drove a red, four-door Hudson with the gear shift lever on the steering column. One Sunday he took us for a joy ride on Memorial Drive along the Charles River. When he reached into the glove compartment for cigarettes I caught sight of a revolver. Dick would favor us with good-sized ends of meat for my mother's gravy and did not ask for ration stamps. She told me it was horse meat.

We got a telephone that year, which frequently rang with Nellie whispering on the phone asking my mother to come over — Dick was threatening. My mother was very self-assured. She was taller than my father, and ample. Her job at the MGH had accustomed her to dealing with people under stress. She did not engage Dick on these occasions, but sat down and had a cup of tea with Nellie. Dick would calm down and usually leave, violence averted.

My baby brother, Joey, arrived in March, 1942. Doctor Romberg, a physician from the MGH, made house calls. My mother was busy with the baby and my father constantly worked. He took any job, including shoveling snow from midnight to 5AM clearing the railroad tracks at North Station. I had my freedom.

After school I visited a lot with my best friend in the class, Lee Wee Yen. His parents were the proprietors of a Chinese hand laundry on Temple Street, a few blocks away. Lee Wee would lead me through the curtains to the back of the store, where we cracked open bright red leechee nuts until his father nodded to him to help a customer. Then, I would cross Cambridge Street to the children's room on the lower level of the West End Branch Public Library in the Old West Church. Fanny Goldstein, the librarian, saw my interest, and took me upstairs to the adult section of the library, where I browsed around the stacks and found the Encyclopedia Britannica.

When school closed in June for the summer the newspapers tacked to our bathroom door had photographs of Panzer tanks in the African desert and General Rommel in goggles.

Stickball, Stukas, Symphonies

When they heard my father's whistle the kids at the stickball game shouted "Hey, Frankie, your father wants you." There were always kids waiting to get into the game, so my leaving was no problem.

In the summer of 1942 I usually headed for the Blackstone School playground, where I could almost always find neighborhood kids in a game of stickball, or playing handball against the school wall, or "Chinese" — handball with a bounce. There were hide-and-seek type games which involved beating on the one who was "it," such as Beat the Bear, and Buck, Buck, How Many Fingers Up? The most popular game was Ringolivio. Two captains would each pick kids for his side. Any number could be on a team. One team scattered and hid, and after a long count the other team had to find and capture the others and take them to "base." The game could go on all day and after dark, with kids drifting in and out. The whistle was my signal to leave.

My father tightened his lips, curled his tongue against his teeth, compressed his diaphragm and produced a piercing whistle, three distinctive notes, repeated twice, that carried for more than a block. His Eaton Street store was only a few doors away from the "Blackie's" cement school yard, and he would whistle for me at the end of the day to meet him at the store and go home for supper. Even if I was beyond earshot I was certain to hear from a passerby: "Frankie, your father's calling you." I always obeyed. My parents could count on me. They trusted me.

Neisner's Five and Ten Cent Store on Washington Street in downtown Boston had a model airplane section. I used to launch balsa wood gliders from the hills on the Boston Common, and now was the time to put together a real model airplane. I chose the Stuka dive bomber model airplane kit made by the Guillow company.

The kit was very complicated. The Stuka had inverted gull wings, requiring assembly in four sections with joiners at the V. The fixed landing gear had streamlined "pants" covering the wheels. The cockpit was an intricate birdcage. I used a razor blade to cut each rib, spar, joiner and stringer from the patterns printed on flat balsa sheets. The cutting job was monumental; there were hundreds of individual, numbered pieces.

Gluing the balsa cutouts to form the individual sections of the fuselage and wings was even more complex. I laid wax paper over the pattern so that when glued the pieces would not stick to it. Each component had to be secured with common pins to hold it while the glue dried. The tension from curved stringers soon pulled the pieces apart and I had to try again. The task proved impossible. The Stuka defeated me. I gave up. I had better luck with a simpler model, a Piper Cub, which, when assembled and painted, I hung from the ceiling by strings attached to the wingtips and tail.

On summer evenings I headed for the Hatch Memorial Shell on the Esplanade, where members of the Boston Pops Orchestra gave free outdoor concerts, Arthur Fiedler conducting. My mother provided me with an old blanket to sit on. I would get there early, lay the blanket on the grass close to the bandshell, and ask someone to watch it for me while I went fishing with a hand line off a nearby boat dock. On my return from one of those fishing expeditions I found my blanket on a wooden folding chair that rented for ten cents. Mr. Cheever, who arrived early each evening and set his chair in the first row, had observed my routine and rented a chair for me. I thanked him and asked him if he wanted any of my fish. He declined. Each evening I sat next to Mr. Cheever, whom I impressed with the story of my violin lessons with Stacia Romanoff, and my familiarity with the composers whose names were affixed to the frieze at the front base of the Hatch Shell: Strauss, Schumann, Debussy, Gluck, Chopin, Ravel, Wagner, Weber, Rimsky-Korsakov, Verdi, Hayden, Monteverdi, Dvorak, Liszt, Beethoven, Rachmaninoff, Bach, Grieg, Mozart, Tchaikovsky, Bizet, Handel, Mendelsohn, Brahms, Franck, Saint-Saens, Rossini, Schubert, Berlioz, Offenbach, Gounod.

Mr. Cheever winced at Arthur Fiedler's conducting and concert choices. He said that Fiedler was as stiff as a general — an automaton. His selections were martial — lots of Richard Wagner full of kettle drums and clash cymbals, Tchaikovsky's 1812 Overture complete with chimes and cannons, and Sousa marches. I thought the concerts were great, but understood Mr. Cheever's point.

When I told my parents about Mr. Cheever they said I should invite him to our house for pastries. He accepted. He lived only a few blocks away, on Chestnut Street at the top of Beacon Hill. He took a small anisette cookie with his tea. I played Schubert's "Ave Maria" for him, my mother's favorite, a very easy piece with simple fingering and bowing. Mr. Cheever complimented me and was very appreciative of the visit. My parents were proud of me.

At the Kitchen Table

By the end of the summer of 1942 I was permitted to go outside the range of my father's whistle, so long as I came home in time for supper. My mother was occupied with my baby brother, Joey, and my father was constantly working — at his WPA job days, and evenings in his store assembling the toys and novelties he peddled on weekends. I used my freedom to venture alone into familiar territory such as the Esplanade, Boston Common, the Public Garden, and Washington Street downtown, then further, through the North End to the Boston waterfront, where chandlery windows displayed deep sea divers' helmets, suits, and weighted boots. I walked out onto the piers to watch fishermen on their boats.

My exploring ended as the days shortened and it got colder. After school I spent more time at the West End Branch Library, where librarian Fanny Goldstein kept a watchful eye over me. At the Heath Christian Center, Reverend Mario Cestaro and his wife, Mary Alice, opened their doors to neighborhood children. It felt like home. I joined the Drama Club and the Chorus. My greatest performance was in the Christmas Show, where I hammed up "The Yellow Rose of Texas," strutting the stage wearing a straw hat and twirling a walking stick.

When winter set in, family activity was concentrated in the kitchen. My parents kept the oil heaters in the other rooms on the lowest possible setting. A bath consisted of pots of boiling water poured into the bathtub. The next morning, any remaining water droplets had turned into ice crystals. Water in pans placed on the fire escape became ice for our ice box.

Putting good food on the table was never in question, but one's plate had to be cleaned; the admonition for not doing so: "Think of all the starving children in Africa." Whenever friends or relatives appeared unannounced, out came capicola, pepperoni, salami, Romano cheese and seeded bread, followed by my father's favorite: coffee with a shot of anisette — excellent for dunking hard biscotti.

On Saturdays my mother took my little brother and me to Cambridge to visit her parents. We boarded the el at the Charles Street Station, where it emerged from the subway. The tracks ran in the center of the Longfellow Bridge across the Charles River, then descended into the subway on the Cambridge side, where we got off at Central Square. While grandma Arcangela pounded out her pasta dough and sampled her spaghetti sauce, I wound up the Victrola and listened to recordings of Enrico Caruso, and of Bing Crosby singing "Red Sails in the Sunset."

Sunday dinner was at my father's parents on Prince Street in the North End. We could smell the frying garlic and onions even before we entered the building. My grandmother Rosa was cooking lamb, pork and sausages brought to her by the workmen whose injuries she had splinted and bandaged that morning.

On our return we picked up copies of suburban newspapers at the North Station; my mother would scan these for information about parades where my father could peddle.

Approaching Christmas season the kitchen table was covered with bunches of evergreen sprigs, red holly berries, gold and silver ribbon, and silver bells. My parents arranged these into corsages held together with wire; a hatpin at the back attached the corsage to a lady's coat lapel. My father sold the corsages in front of downtown department stores. Although peddling was prohibited in the area, an understanding police officer would usually let my father alone until a sergeant came along. For Easter, my parents filled wicker baskets with candy eggs and chocolate Easter bunnies wrapped in cellophane, and attached bows to the handles. I was enlisted to help my father tote these to his best sales spot — the Newbury Street entrance to the Public Garden. My mother counted the coins from the day's receipts on the kitchen table, rolled them tightly in paper, and hid them at the back of the bottom drawer of their bedroom bureau.

In the spring of 1943 I was a ten year old fifth-grader eager to please my teacher, Miss Magner. I won a Boston School Department district spelling bee in my grade category and had an engraved medal attached to a red white and blue ribbon to prove it. My idea for a class project — a display of seed packets for planting in Victory Gardens — rated a center section photo in the Boston Daily Record. Intent on being the first to answer Miss Magner's questions, I raised my hand before she finished asking them. She looked elsewhere in the room for someone to answer, but I knew I was her favorite.

The newspapers tacked to the bathroom door had headlines about the Jewish Uprising in the Warsaw Ghetto.

The Great Spirit

The Egyptian Room in the basement of the Boston Museum of Fine Arts was a cool place to escape the heat on a summer Sunday afternoon. We took the streetcar from Scollay Square subway station and got off at the Huntington Avenue entrance to the museum. There, in bronze turned green by the elements, an Indian brave sat bareback on his colt, gazing to the heavens, arms outstretched and palms up, in an eternal "Appeal to the Great Spirit."

The corridors leading to the basement galleries were lined with paintings, buddhas, textiles, Chinese drawings, and entire rooms from the Colonial era. In the basement, after passing through a gallery of Greek and Etruscan vases and sculptures, we entered a large room filled with massive stone sarcophagi, mummies, and funerary of gold necklaces, jeweled collars, carved animals, and scarabs. All was silent. No one even whispered.

I recognized some of the collections from catalogues Boris Mirski had given me. Boris was the proprietor of a small picture-framing shop in a basement store on Charles Street. He had presented my parents with an etching of Saint Theresa, "The Little Flower," and one of Saint Anthony, on dark wood inlaid with gold leaf. Gold leaf halos circled their heads. He gave me a copy of the museum's Catalogue of Paintings and its Catalogue of Greek and Roman Sculpture.

Boris and his wife Aida were my parents' dearest friends. Both couples got married the same year, 1928, and moved into adjacent flats at

21 Eaton Street. Boris and Aida had no money. Their kitchen furniture consisted of a wooden table and fruit crates for chairs. Boris's payment from the struggling artists he befriended at his frame shop was usually non monetary — a gift of a painting. My father had opened a small fruit store in a basement on Chambers Street, but, because of his poor business judgment, it did not last long. Instead of sneaking a spoiled tomato into the bag of tomatoes he weighed out for a customer, as all the merchants did, he put spoiled fruit aside. While it lasted, however, Aida and Adeline had plenty of soft tomatoes, old cabbage, wilted lettuce, squishy zucchini and other rejects, which they combined with meat bones to cook up heavily spiced stews that kept everybody happy.

Aida Mirski was the only person who could compete with my mother and my aunt Mary in the laughter and screaming department. Aida was a "Fortunato" — a large, happy, Italian Catholic family that loved to cook and loved to eat. Demonstrative, bosomy Aida Fortunato married Boris Mirski, a short, paunchy, prematurely balding Jew with a little moustache, a perpetually furrowed brow, and a worried look. No matter the circumstances, Aida was joyful and festive; Boris was quiet. Aida was my father's best audience, exploding in laughter at his oft-repeated jokes. Although Boris sat sphinx-like, we knew that he was totally taken with Aida; his sidelong glances and winks revealed all. Aida adopted Judaism, outdoing everyone at being Jewish, especially with the feasts, where she was joined in the merriment by her sister Clara, Henry and Esther Mazer, Boris, Aunty Gittel, Arthur Forte, Mary Lanciano, Frank and Adeline.

THE SUMMER OF 1943 Reverend Cestaro and his wife, Mary Alice, were watching over twelve kids from the West End attending the Pond Homestead Baptist Camp in Wrentham, courtesy of the Boston Baptist Mission. Reverend Cestaro slept downstairs, keeping an eye on six boys on folding cots; Mary Alice bunked upstairs with six girls.

There had been talk in the neighborhood about the camp. Mrs. Jackman, very prominent in the Women's Sodality at St. Joseph's

Church, came to our apartment to talk to my mother about her enrolling me in the camp. There was definite animus among the Catholic clergy about the Baptist settlement house only a block from St. Joseph's. Mrs. Jackman told my mother she respected her decision and understood the opportunity being offered — the Catholics had no such activities for kids — but was curious about her plans for my religious upbringing. My mother assured her that I was a good Catholic and would be preparing for my Confirmation. The church's Irish lay establishment had good reason to wonder about the Del Vecchios ever since my father's coup in seizing control of Sunday mass collections.

Days at the camp began with putting up the cots, cereal for breakfast, and Chapel, where Reverend Cestaro told us Bible stories and we sang hymns, Mary Alice on the organ. We played games outside, or did crafts if it rained, such as making lanyards with gimp. Afternoons, Rev. Cestaro drove us to the Wrentham Town pond, which let us in without charging the ten cent entry fee. This was his first year behind the wheel of a vehicle, so he drove in slow motion, which was about all that "Jeremiah," an old truck fitted out with benches to serve as a bus, could handle. Nights were the most fun. After dinner we had free time, then gathered closely around Reverend Cestaro who had stoked up a log fire in the camp's huge fieldstone fireplace, where he would read us spine-chilling stories. "The Wendigo" was the scariest. From a book with dog-eared pages he read the story of a hunting party in the distant northern woods of Canada, stalked by the Wendigo — a creature of different animal forms that drags hunters from tents as they sleep. The Indians knew of its presence by its scent. The Wendigo's feet become fiery because of the incredible speed at which it carries its victims through the forest: *"Oh! oh! My feet of fire! My burning feet of fire!"*

One afternoon, the bus that was supposed to pick us up at the town pond broke down, necessitating a two mile walk back to camp. As we were leaving, Vera Stachisin lagging behind, exchanged a glance with me, and I dropped back to join her. We had played games, gone to Chapel, had meals together, and sat by the fire scared by the Wendigo, but we had never actually talked to each other. We did little talking on this walk, but it was different. There was a feeling about it. Vera was from a Ukrainian family who lived on Kinnard Avenue in the West End. Although Italians and Jews were in the majority, with Irish close behind, the neighborhood had plenty of Greeks, Poles, Ukrainians and foreign accents you heard in the neighborhood stores. Vera was taller than me, with dark hair. We had left the road to walk along the railroad tracks. It was warm and quiet. The grasshoppers bounced out of our way ahead of us. The sound of insects buzzing was distinct. I thought about kissing Vera, but didn't. When camp was over, and I was back in the West End, I walked down to Kinnard Avenue hoping to see Vera on the street. One day she came out of her door, but became very nervous when she saw me. Glancing up to see if her mother was at the window, she motioned me to follow her. On a bench in the Esplanade Vera delivered the kiss we had both been waiting for.

Chapter 4

Making The Grade

An animated conversation in Italian was underway by a group of men gathered around the pinball machine at the back of Pat Piccolomini's store at the corner of Snow Hill and Prince Streets in the North End, across from my grandparent's. Pat's lemon slush was a favorite on hot summer days but his main draw was the number pool. There were always guys hanging out in the store placing bets and playing pinball. My father had taken me for a slush this Sunday afternoon in August, 1943, and joined the conversation at the back. When we left, he explained that the men were concerned about relatives in Italy. During the summer, the newspapers carried stories of Allied bombings of airfields in Palermo and Messina in Sicily, and Naples on the Italian peninsula. The Allies were en route from victories in Africa to an invasion of Italy. Those who had supported Mussolini now had a different tune. The North End had been the destination of many immigrants from Sicily and the poor regions of the Italian south. My father's family emigrated from Avellino, a province east of Naples and north of Salerno — two obvious targets for invasion. There were many worried paisanos in the North End.

Soon after I began Mr. O'Brien's sixth grade class at the Peter Faneuil School in September, the newspaper pages my father tacked to the bathroom door showed arrows from the north coast of Africa and from Sicily pointing at the Gulf of Salerno and at Naples. The Allies' amphibious assault on the Italian mainland had begun.

Mr. O'Brien was the only male teacher at the Peter Faneuil School. He was a tall, dignified, courtly man, slightly balding, with a moustache. He was always impeccably dressed. I felt very comfortable in his class, more at ease than I had been with my previous teachers. Miss Magner, fifth grade, was a disciplinarian. She used the rattan if a boy showed any defiance. She would summon the disrespectful boy to the coatroom behind the side blackboard and administer three or four whacks of the cane to his palm. Only the wimpiest kids would make a sound. Miss Magner was a piece of cake for me. All it took was to appear attentive. Miss Sullivan, fourth grade, was a problem. She was old, fat, ugly, and displeased with everyone. No amount of obsequiousness or scholarship made a difference. The main advantage of her class was that she never removed her fat butt from her chair. She also was hard of hearing. These two complementary attributes meant a student could do anything he wanted at his desk without her knowing the difference. Grades one, two and three didn't matter much in the rebellion department. We were still little boys.

Early in the school year Mr. O'Brien announced that if anyone was interested in going to Boston Latin School for the seventh grade he should bring a note from his parents.

He explained that in order to be admitted, a student would have to score well in a citywide competitive exam, or get all A's in the sixth grade. After the Peter Faneuil, the next school in succession would have been William Blackstone Junior High, the "Blackie," definitely a step to academic oblivion. The Peter Faneuil was located on Beacon Hill and included in its radius the section of the West End in which we lived. The other elementary schools in the West End, the Winchell and the Mayhew, were definitely sub par. Several of us brought in notes from our parents endorsing our candidacies for Boston Latin School. I set out to get all A's.

I was encouraged in this goal by my cousin Cyrus Del Vecchio. Cyrus was a couple of years older than me, and in his second year at Boston Latin School when I entered the sixth grade. Cyrus, and his older brother, Michael, lived nearby on McLean Street facing St. Joseph's church, in the nicest apartment building in the West End. It was impressive. Unlike every other building in the neighborhood, where there were no barriers to entry, the entrance door inside their entry alcove was locked.

The handles on the doors were shiny brass, as were the mailboxes in the entry. The marble tiles in the entry were kept spotless. Even when slush was tracked in from the street a janitor soon cleaned them. The inside stairway was marble with brass railings. Their apartment was large, airy, and well furnished. Cyrus's father operated a shoe repair business and his mother owned real estate. Although his family and my father's were from the same town in Italy, which was full of Del Vecchios, their backgrounds were very different. His family owned property. My father's parents lived on the second floor of a tiny house, their animals below.

Cyrus took it upon himself to give me worldly advice. He saw that I was on my own, venturing far afield on the streets of Boston and hanging out with the neighborhood kids at Charlie Maccarone's store, playing the pinball machine. Even before Mr. O'Brien asked who in his sixth grade class would be interested in going to Boston Latin School, Cyrus had delivered a stern lecture to me — from a twelve-year old to a ten-year old. He said that if I didn't do something about where I was headed I would end up at the Blackie, but if I worked hard at school I could get into Boston Latin. I really didn't need the lecture, for my parents had been beating that message into my head forever — Get an education. Nonetheless, the encouragement was timely, for now I had to get to work.

One day the following spring Mr. O'Brien handed out envelopes in the class, one of which was addressed to me. It was a letter from the Boston School Department informing me of my academic admission to Boston Latin School. I did not have to take the exam.

Carny

"The Boston Shows" was a crooked carnival outfit; the carnies were grifters, drunks and cheats. The carny set up on vacant sites around Boston, generally on Friday, pay day, and was gone without a trace before daybreak on Monday. Here today, gone tomorrow. Most of the locations were in the poor communities ringing Boston — Chelsea, Revere,

Everett, Somerville, South Medford, East Cambridge, usually near a trolley line. This enabled my father to get there and set up a novelty stand. In the summer of 1944, at age eleven, I was old enough and strong enough to carry his goods and help him at the stand. I *had* to help him — it was impossible for him to carry enough merchandise alone; he had to have someone mind the stand when he went to the bathroom or needed a break, and to watch out for stealing. I hated it. My freedom was gone. I could have been hanging out with the kids on the corner or been on my own. I hoped for rain, so that we wouldn't go; but my father would always go on the chance it would clear up. Although I was happy when the day got rained out so we could leave, my father would be upset. His WPA job had ended long ago; this was the way he made a living. Not only did a rain out mean he had lost income for the day, he had also lost the day's "nut," the money he paid the carny owner for the novelty concession.

We left our house early and went to my father's store to get his wares: a badgeboard wrapped in oilcloth to protect it from rain, a peddler's wicker basket packed with novelties, and a hand pump for inflating balloons. We lugged these up Cambridge Street to the Bowdoin Square subway station and made the train changes and transfers necessary to get to the carny location. My father was not a carny. He was not one of them. He knew their game and disapproved of it. He kept his distance from the carnies and they ignored him. The entire carny was an enterprise to relieve the suckers of their dough. My father was among the very few there who weren't crooks. He sold balloons and novelties at a fair price; the carnies cheated everyone. The other honest locations were the hot dog truck, the ice cream stand and the cotton candy wagon. The rides were on the level, but most of the guys who operated them were drunks. Other than the food vendors, my father had no natural allies on the lot; however, they were too busy watching out for themselves just as he had to, to be of any help to one another. My father did alright at his novelty concession. Parents could at least buy their kids something tangible — a balloon, a pinwheel, a bird with a tail that rotated when the bird was twirled on a string, making a chirping sound. A young fellow could buy his girl a button imprinted with a comical saying and hung with a heart locket and a cute teddy bear.

When it wasn't busy, which was most of the day, I had free run of the carnival and watched how the carnies operated. The key to separating someone from his cash was to create the impression that he could win. This was the job of the shill, the "outside man." The pitchman — the "inside man" — would display a flash of prizes high on shelves of the booth — "the joint": huge stuffed animals, dolls dressed in satin gowns, glittering costume jewelry displayed on black satin. The shill would start playing a game, lose by a hair, but get closer and closer on each try. A crowd would form, and gasps would go up when the shill just missed. When excitement was high, the shill would win, claim a prize from the top shelf, and circulate around the carnival with it. The guy next in line would be some poor sucker trying to win a big doll for his girlfriend, forking over more and more cash as he got closer to winning, but just missing each time. When he ultimately gave up or went broke, the carny would hand the girl a cheap stuffed animal as a consolation prize.

The real thievery took place at the gambling games. The joints were rigged with wires controlled by pedals and handles. The shills were on the alert for a mark — usually someone with money who thought he could outsmart the guys running the booth. The mark would be suckered in by being allowed at first to win small amounts. Encouraged, he would go for double or nothing, developing confidence, but then lose by a hair. He was hooked. He coughed up more and more of his own dough in a cycle of doubling his bets, until he took the final plunge and lost. At this point the mark would realize he had been fleeced, and was ready to be violent. The carnies had anticipated this moment, and formed a circle behind him as he was getting deeper into the scam. They would elbow the mark away from the joint, and if necessary, engage him in a shoving match or a fight, and a cop would eject him from the grounds.

FOLLOWING MASS ONE Sunday in late August, 1944, members of the Roma Band began assembling on Thacher Street in the North End in front of St. Mary's Church. They wore green uniforms, red carnations pinned to the lapels. The bass drum displayed the green, white and red-striped Italian flag. The elderly, mustachioed gentlemen of the band began warming up on their instruments in preparation for leading a procession sponsored by a society of paisani from the Avellino region. Members of the society were readying a statue of the Virgin Mary to carry on a pallet around the North End Streets, seeking donations. I was helping my father set up his novelty stand.

These Italian fiestas had been growing every year since the 1920's, organized by immigrants from various regions of Italy who formed fraternal societies in their North End neighborhoods. In 1942, with the U.S. at war with the Axis powers, the fiestas were cancelled, as were those in the summer of 1943. In the fall of 1943 the Italians surrendered to the Allies, and in June 1944, the Germans were routed from Rome. The largest society, Montefalcione, whose fiesta around St. Leonard's Church was the most successful, decided it was still too early to resume the celebrations.

The St. Mary's society event triggered resentment in the community, and there was little festive spirit around its handful of pushcarts offering raw quahogs, nuts, strings of figs, Italian grinders, and "snowballs" — shaved ice sweetened with colored syrups. We sold a few balloons but little else. When the fiesta was over, I had a couple of weeks of freedom before starting Boston Latin School.

Frank Del Vecchio

SCHOLA LATINA BOSTONIENSIS

"Gallia est omnis divisa in partes tres, quarum unam incolunt Belgae, aliam Aquitani, tertiam qui ipsorum lingua Celtae, nostra Galli appellantur. Hi omnes lingua, institutis, legibus inter se differunt. Gallos ab Aquitanis Garumna flumen, a Belgis Matrona et Sequana dividit."[1]

COMMENTARII DE BELLO GALLICO,
Gaius Julius Caesar, (100 BC — 44BC)

"*YE CALL ME chief.* . ." boomed Cyrus Del Vecchio's voice, commanding the attention of the students filling the Boston Latin School auditorium — "*and ye do well to call **him** chief who for twelve long years has met upon the arena every shape of man or beast the broad Empire of Rome could furnish, and who never yet lowered his arm.*" Not a murmur, a cough, or a rustle of programs disturbed his explosive delivery of the classic oration "Spartacus to the Gladiators at Capua."

"*. . . If there be one among you who can say that ever, in public fight or private brawl, my actions did belie my tongue, let him stand forth and say it. If there be three in all your company dare face me on the bloody sands, let them come on.*"

Cyrus could just as well have been standing in the Coliseum two thousand years earlier throwing down this challenge to the assembled students as delivering a declamation in 1944. The three-hundred year tradition of the Boston Latin School, founded in 1635, the first public school in America, guaranteed the disciplined attention of the student body. The names engraved along the upper frieze of the auditorium carried the names of five signers of the Declaration of Independence who had been students: John Hancock, Samuel Adams, Benjamin Franklin, Robert Treat Paine, William Hooper. The curriculum of Latin, Greek,

---

1   *All Gaul is divided into three parts, one of which the Belgae inhabit, the Aquitani another, those who in their own language are called Celts, in our Gauls, the third. All these differ from each other in language, customs and laws.*

German, French, history and mathematics ensured only the most serious pedagogy in the classrooms.

My cousin Cyrus was not the only Del Vecchio on the Declamation program this day. His older brother, Michael, recited Clarence Darrow's plea for the defense in the murder trial of labor radical William Haywood —

> *"Gentlemen, it is not for him alone that I speak. I speak for the poor, for the weak, for the weary, for that long line of men who in darkness and despair have borne the labors of the human race. The eyes of the world are upon you, upon you twelve men of Idaho tonight. . ."*

Cyrus encouraged, no, ordered me to register for the next Declamation contest. Declamation, rhetoric, oratory, was one of the three classical disciplines of discourse: grammar — the tools of language; logic — the use of reasoning; rhetoric — the art of persuasion. Cyrus and Michael were intent on inspiring me to scholarship. I did not have the force of Cyrus or the sensitivity of Michael, but I did not hesitate. The stage of the Boston Latin School auditorium would give me an opportunity to perform.

CYRUS WAS DISAPPOINTED in my choice. It was an exercise in acting, not rhetoric — a dramatic reading of Edgar Allan Poe's "The Tell-Tale Heart."

> *"TRUE! nervous, very, very dreadfully nervous I had been and am; but why WILL you say that I am mad? The disease had sharpened my senses, not destroyed, not dulled them. Above all was the sense of hearing acute. I heard all things in the heaven and in the earth. I heard many things in hell. How then am I mad? Hearken! and observe how healthily, how calmly, I can tell you the whole story. . ."*

The speaker's logic demonstrates his homicidal madness. My delivery was as sinister as character actor Peter Lorre's. Although it pleased the audience and I scored high with the judges, Cyrus was concerned that I was more interested in drama than in scholarship.

WHILE I WAS learning to conjugate verbs and decline nouns the Allies were battling the Axis in Europe and in the Pacific. Since D-Day, June 6, 1944, Allied forces squeezed the German Empire from the west. The Soviet Red Army was decimating the German military from the east. On April 12, 1945, President Roosevelt died; April 29, Mussolini was killed by partisans and hung by the feet in a square in Milan; Hitler killed himself April 30. On May 7, 1945 — "VE Day" — Germany surrendered. Japan, however, resisted suicidally. The U.S dropped an atomic bomb on Hiroshima August 6, and on Nagasaki August 9. On August 15, 1945 — "VJ Day" — the Japanese surrendered. World War II was over.

Spooked

An odor of whiskey and formaldehyde greeted those entering the stairwell at 75 Chambers Street, where we moved in 1945. The formaldehyde was from the undertaking parlor on the first floor; the whisky from its proprietor, mortician John B. Burke.

Burke was one of the many politically-connected undertakers in Boston favored with unclaimed corpses from city morgues: the "Southern Mortuary," at Boston City Hospital in the South End, and the "Northern Mortuary," on North Grove Street next to the Massachusetts General Hospital, a few blocks from 75 Chambers.

Burke had only sporadic business since the great Coconut Grove Nightclub Fire of 1942, when more than 100 of the 490 fatalities were processed at the MGH morgue. I rarely saw a Mortuary wagon there during the summer. There was more activity in the winter — I expect from winos too drunk to go to one of the missions.

One day Jimmy Delmont asked me if I had ever gone into Burke's. I said I hadn't. We looked in the storefront window. It was dark inside. "No sign of life," said Jimmy, the comedian. I knew what was coming. "Let's take a look," he said.

At the back of the hallway there was a door leading to the cellar. Inside the stairway it was total blackness. Each step creaked. We moved cautiously, ears cocked to find out if we had been heard. The door at the bottom was not locked. A small amount of light came through a window at the far end. After a few minutes our eyes adapted and we could make out objects. The room was cluttered with chairs and furniture. Funeral vases and religious statuettes were stacked on tables. A few caskets were on shelves along the cellar walls. Just as we reached the back wall there was a sound. Someone was opening the upstairs door. The stairwell light came on. Footsteps. The door to the cellar opened. Silhouetted against the light from the stairway I saw that it was Burke, the undertaker.

There was nowhere we could hide. We stood motionless. Burke switched on a flashlight and moved slowly around the room looking for something. He was heading directly toward where we were located. When he was only a few feet away, his flashlight beam found us. We were petrified. Burke stopped about an arm's length from where we stood. He swept the light over us, from our shoes to our frozen faces. He looked right at us, staring wordlessly for two or three minutes. What was he thinking? I sensed that for Burke, this was not an unfamiliar moment; undoubtedly, alone each day with his corpses and his whiskey, he had seen apparitions before. Then, Burke turned, headed for the cellar door, and disappeared up the stairs. We made a rapid retreat as soon as his footsteps died away. I never again ventured into Burke the Undertaker.

The Fast Break

In the mid-Forties the two-handed set shot was how you put a basketball through the hoop. A player set his feet, grasped the ball with both hands, and propelled it towards the spot near the gym's ceiling where the downward slope of the ball's parabolic arc would end at the basket. That technique did not work in the low ceiling of the Heath Christian Center gym, the chapel which Reverend Mario Cestaro converted to a basketball court. The ball would hit the ceiling because of the high arc required. The only chance of sinking a basket was to throw or "push" the ball with one hand on a low trajectory just over the rim, or angle it off the backboard. Neighborhood boys began to use the push shot in pick up games at the sandy lot at the bottom of Chambers Street. Sonny Grasso and the kids who worked with him in his family's oil and ice delivery business played at the lot after work and got good at these shots.

Sonny Grasso, with his friends Sammy and Johnny Marinella, Domenic DiFruscio, Frankie Fazzina, Ben Tankle, and Shawney Marshall lugged two five-gallon cans of heating oil weighing more than thirty-five pounds each up tenement stairs, or a fifty or even one-hundred pound block of ice held by tongs against a rubber cape over their back. After a summer doing this they were the strongest kids in the neighborhood. They ran everyone into the ground at the sandlot basketball games.

"Lefty" Fivozinsky saw Sonny Grasso's team play and encouraged them to join the West End House Boys Club, where he coached. "Lefty" Fivozinsky was one of a couple of dozen men, mostly Jewish, who volunteered their time after work to coach at the boys club. The West End House had been built with funds from the estate of James Jackson Storrow. This was another legacy of the Boston Brahmins. The building at 16 Blossom Street had a full sized basketball court on the second floor. A large game room with ping pong tables and card tables was on the first floor. Meeting rooms, showers and lockers were in the basement. The team named itself "The Storrows." Lefty Fivozinsky became the coach. I joined their club.

Every club at the West End House was required to adopt rules of procedure, hold regular meetings and keep minutes. Members took part in all the club's activities. One of these was a declamation contest in the spring. My team expected great things of me since I was an experienced Latin School declaimer. However, spring was a long time off. Basketball was the activity in the winter. Coach Lefty Fivo had developed a theory about the game, and the Storrows were going to demonstrate it.

In the mid-Forties the game of basketball was orchestrated like football. There were set formations and set plays. The team with possession of the ball took assigned positions on the far court and the defending team formed a rigid "zone" defense. Offense favored players who could sink set shots. Defense favored tall players with long arms. Lefty's theory was that speed could defeat set formations by getting players downcourt before the opponents could form into a zone. The Storrows may have been short — Dom DiFruscio, at center, the tallest at five feet eight — but they were fast. Lefty's tactic was a "fast break." Whoever got the ball was to dribble it as fast as he could towards the opponent's end of the court, and everyone else on the team was to run as fast as possible towards the opponent's basket. The defensive zone would not have a chance to set — a quick bounce pass to the fastest Storrow on the fast break should produce a lay-up basket. If the opposing team converged around the basket, the bounce pass would go to a clear player who would get off a quick push shot. At our end of the court, instead of a zone defense we played "man to man." Each defender picked up the opponent closest to him as early as possible and crowded him all the way down court. The dribbler was hassled by constant attempts at stealing the ball.

These tactics exhausted our bigger opponents, who could not outrun a bunch of kids who had been carrying fifty pound blocks of ice all summer up five flights of tenement stairs. They might try for a while, but this was tiring, required frequent substitutions, and disrupted a team's rhythm. The Storrows frustrated teams that were bigger and stronger than us.

By the spring of 1946 the Storrows had gained a reputation with their fast break style of play. We were invited to play an exhibition game at the Roxbury Boys Club against a group of boys our own age. The stands were packed. We went onto the court first, practiced dribbles and lay-ups, then sat on our bench. Out came the home team, an impressive bunch of Black athletes, taller than us. They were fluid in their warmup. It was obvious we didn't have a chance.

Our fast breaks, Sammy Marinella's behind the back passes, Fazzina's push shots, and DiFruscio's hook shots weren't enough to overcome their organized play in the first period. As the second period ended we had made up a few points with our speed, but were still behind. In the dressing room at the half, Lefty Fivozinsky was intense. He announced that we would beat them — that the Roxbury team would fold before the end of the second half; that they would not be able to keep up with us as long as we kept driving. He gave Ben Tankle and me an assignment. He rarely sent us onto the court unless the Storrows were way ahead, but this night he put us in at the start of the third period, with orders to run as fast as we could as long as we could and throw our opponents off their game — rattle them. I got away with a couple of elbows and collisions before the referee recognized what was going on and ejected me. Ben Tankle did the same. We had done our job. We had agitated the opposing players, who retaliated, and got into foul trouble.

At the third period time out, Lefty ordered the Storrows to *run*. We briefly took the lead, and the crowd quieted. The other team, however, regained its composure, settled into its defensive pattern, frustrated our hustling, and won. Their players said "Good game" as we went through the obligatory end of game handshakes. Back at the West End House we won in our age division. The other coaches adopted Lefty's tactics. Soon, the Brenners and the Hawks were running up and down the court at a frantic pace, dribbling low, making behind the back passes, and rifling the ball towards the basket. Nobody took a set shot anymore.

Chapter 5

Street Smart

My fourth attempt at Catholic sanctification failed when, at age twelve, I was administered the sacrament of Confirmation by Archbishop Richard Cushing in a ceremony at Saint Joseph's Roman Catholic Church. The previous sacraments I had received, Baptism, Communion, and Penance, had not succeeded in inculcating in me the requisite faith. Confirmation is intended to close the deal. You are to receive the Holy Spirit. I knelt at the altar rail under false pretenses, for I was in a state of detachment about the ritual. I only went through the motions. My parents sensed that I was disconnected, but were happy that I completed the obligation.

With this performance over, the challenge was how to escape my mother's watchful eye and avoid going to Sunday mass. Unfortunately for me, our building at 75 Chambers Street was directly opposite St. Joseph's Church. Our fourth floor flat looked down at the church's slate roof and its front steps. On Sundays, my mother, leaning on a pillow she placed on the windowsill, enjoyed watching the faithful as they walked to church in their best clothes. My parents attended the ten o'clock mass. If I accompanied them I would not be able to escape, so I formulated a subterfuge. I went to the nine o'clock mass. I exited 75 Chambers Street, crossed to the church, walked up the church steps and through the front door, my mother watching from above. Once inside, I proceeded rapidly up a side aisle to the altar, entered the vestry and descended the stairway to the lower church, where I exited from the side door on McLean Street. My destination was the nearby Blackstone School schoolyard, where every Sunday morning "Honest John" Mazer ran a crap game.

A group of seven or eight guys huddled at an alcove at the back of the schoolyard. Sometimes "Honest John" asked me to be the lookout. I was too young to play, and, anyway, didn't have any money. If I saw a cop heading towards us I whistled, the dice and cash disappeared, and the guys involved themselves in an animated game of "morra" — "bucking up." Two guys stand opposite each other, one is even, the other odd. On the count of "One, two, three, *shoot!*" they throw out one or two fingers. The sum of the fingers is either odd or even and scored accordingly. When the cop passes, out comes the dice and the cash, and the crap game resumes, the morra charade over.

The shooter lays down coins or bills and someone "covers" the bet. Shooting a seven or an eleven — a "natural" — on the first pass, wins the bet; a deuce — "snake eyes," or a trey or twelve — loses it. Any other number shot on the first pass is the "point," which the shooter has to make on a subsequent pass in order to win. If a seven comes up before making the point, he loses.

The Sunday morning crap games were not like the other games I played in the Blackstone schoolyard. Craps was not a game, it was a fight. There were real victors and losers. A loser might hang around for a minute after he was cleaned out, but soon left, beaten and dejected. The regular winners were the tough guys: Migo and Joe Saia, Frank Camoscio, Teddy Deegan. They pocketed the winnings and left silently. It would have been out of place to be boisterous; nobody had spare cash to lose.

SOMETIMES, INSTEAD OF heading for home after school, I went to the penny arcade on downtown Washington Street and watched guys play the pinball machines. Often, someone who had built up a lot of free games on a machine would tire of it and leave them for a kid standing there. The peepshows had continuous reels which hooked a guy into feeding them dimes. When a reel came around to the beginning of its cycle the viewer might walk away since he had already seen it. I was on the lookout for peepshows I could see for free.

There were kids who hung out in the penny arcade all day. I came in the afternoon, toting my school bookbag. They didn't have bookbags. Occasionally a man would treat one of these kids to games on the pinball machines and to see a peepshow. I moved away when one of these men showed an interest in me. One day a kid about my age whom I had noticed hanging around the arcade came over and talked to me. He asked me if I would be interested in a part-time job after school — that he had some friends who got jobs at an office nearby. I went with him to the Milk Street office of an organization that ran a boys' summer camp. My solicitous friend introduced me to a man I recognized as one of those who hovered around kids at the penny arcade. I said I had too much homework to do and wouldn't be able to work after school.

Runaway

I was not happy working for my father in the summers while the other boys in the neighborhood had their freedom. In the summer of 1946 we traveled to parades with Sal Giacoppi, my mother's older brother. Sal had brought my father into the balloon business soon after his marriage in 1928. My father applied himself and was successful, but Sal didn't, and my father disapproved of him. Sal was a flashy dresser, a good dancer, a big talker, and a ladies' man. He was also a gambler; whatever he made, he bet on the races. His life was a cycle of winning, blowing it, then building up a stake again. Sal took losses philosophically; when he won he was upset that he hadn't bet more.

At the parade site Sal sat in the car studying the *Daily Racing Form* while my father readied the peddlers' baskets. He usually parked near a telephone booth so he could call in a bet on a horse. When the parade ended Sal rushed to the telephone for the race results. He did not wait around to make the last sale, for he was anxious to drop us off and head for the dog track in Revere. I liked traveling with my Uncle Sal. His mind was elsewhere; so was mine. He got us home while it was still light, giving me time to hang out with my friends at Charlie Maccarone's corner store, get a lemon slush, and play the pinball machine.

In the fall I entered the ninth grade, Class IV at Boston Latin School. One day in the spring of 1947, Cyrus and Michael Del Vecchio asked me to substitute for a member of their debating team who had gotten sick. Boston Latin School was challenging the reigning District champions, Brookline High School.

The moderator instructed the teams on the debate rules before a packed Latin School auditorium. Michael Del Vecchio, first up for our side, presented a dry but impeccably logical case challenging the merits of the proposition. When it was Cyrus's turn to speak he took the podium, eyed the room with authority, and galvanized the assembly with his oratory. I was the last speaker. My assignment was to rebut the arguments of the other side. Instead of rationality, however, I employed ridicule — to the delight of the audience but not the judges. We lost. My performance confirmed Cyrus's judgment that I was a hopeless case; that I would dissipate my talents and never distinguish myself as a gentleman or a scholar.

The summer of 1947 was a disaster. My father had a concession with a small traveling circus that made a circuit of towns located near railroad lines running between Boston and Providence. The show set up on isolated lots adjacent to railroad spurs. Friday, Saturday and Sunday I was stuck on the midway next to a merry-go-round and its Wurlitzer organ that ground out the same maddening tunes all day. I spent nights with my father in a cheap hotel room in town. There was nothing romantic about circus life. Performers and pitchmen went through the motions show after show. Most of the circus gang were drunks. I was an unhappy kid.

MY FATHER'S DEMANDS on me continued into the fall, when he invented a new product, the "Sweet Adeline Sugar Pop," an eight-inch diameter lollipop with a variegated swirl pattern, which he wrapped in colored cellophane. They sold as fast as the candy maker could produce them. Their weight and bulk necessitated a new way of doing business for my father. He bought a car, a Willys Jeep two-door station wagon. After school, my job was to wrap the lollipops, securing each with a colored bow, and stack them in wooden crates. During the week he sold them to factory workers as they left work. On Saturdays he headed for wherever he could find a crowd. He needed my help carrying the heavy boxes and making sales. It wasn't until the winter set in, and customers hurried past in the cold, that this ended.

The one bright spot during my Sugar Pop packaging days was Dee, the neighborhood tomboy. Dee hung around the Blackie playground and played ringolivio and beat the bear with the boys. One day she tapped on the window of my father's store while I was at work and asked if she could use the bathroom. She came in again and offered to help me with my work. She told me about her parents' constant arguments. I complained about my father's demands. Dee showed her gratitude for my friendship by introducing me to sex.

In the winter of 1947-1948 I spent less and less time at home. I left for school early, a green book bag slung over my shoulder, and took the trolley to Boston Latin School. After school I often stopped at the Museum of Fine Arts, only a couple of blocks away in the Fens, or took the trolley to the main Boston Public Library in Copley Square. The Museum and the Library were different worlds. I read in the inner courtyard of the library, which was designed as a Renaissance cloister, or in the main reading room, tables piled with books and students' notebooks, and silent except for pages being turned. Sometimes I headed for Scollay Square and the penny arcade.

During the war Scollay Square had been a bustling destination for sailors on the town. They packed the burlesque houses: The Old Howard, *"Always Something Doing,"* the Crawford House, and the Casino Theater. Joe & Nemo *"the Hot Dog Kings,"* across from the Old Howard, had a reputation with the entire Atlantic Fleet. Dozens of bars ringed the square full of girls looking for a good time with the swabbies, who hid their cash in their socks.

Now, the Fleet was gone and the square was on the skids. Jack's Lighthouse was a flophouse. The Rialto Movie Theater was the bottom of the barrel: for a dime a wino could sleep the day away stretched out in an aisle between empty rows of seats. There was still *Always Something Doing* at the Old Howard, but the audiences had dwindled to mostly old men and perverts. One snowy winter day I mustered the courage to go up to the ticket booth. I buttoned up my mackinaw coat, pulled my ear-flaps down, wrapped my scarf around my face, and placed two quarters on the counter. Once inside, I hunched down in a seat, my book bag in my lap as protection, still wrapped up for concealment — unnecessary because it was so dark no one could have spotted me. The comedians went mechanically through their routines, with no reaction from the handful in the audience. A few musicians emerged from below the stage and played a flourish for the first stripper, who performed a classic tease with a chair as a prop. When I left the Old Howard I felt guilty that I had wasted my time and not done my homework.

Cyrus made one last try with me. He encouraged me to go out for winter track. He was a good high jumper and hurdler. I was too short. He said I should do the 50-yard dash and the standing broad jump. The Boston Latin School track team was ready to accept any volunteer, so I was issued indoor track shoes, running shorts, a "BLS" jersey, and a sweat suit. We practiced by running around the school's basement corridors. The track meets were held in the Boston armories, where the Black athletes from Boston Trade School, the High School of Commerce, and Roxbury Memorial dominated. I had the distinction of finishing last in every competition. No matter how hard I practiced the standing broad jump I could never attain my goal of hitting the eight foot mark.

As the winter was ending and the feel of spring was in the air I knew what was coming.

I had turned fifteen and my father was making a calendar for the summer. With his new mobility he had plans for parades for all the holidays, and a schedule of town fairs and charitable organizations' field days. He had arranged with the Italian Societies for concessions at the North End fiestas in August and September. I made a decision; I was not going to stay around to work for my father. I contrived a diversion, hinting to classmates that I might head for New York City. No one took me seriously.

On a Sunday afternoon in June, at home alone, I packed a suitcase, took the money my father had hidden in the bottom drawer of their bureau, and left a note addressed to my mother, referring to my father as "your husband," telling her that I had taken the money, that I was going out on my own and she should not worry. I walked down the stairs, out of 75 Chambers Street, and headed for downtown Boston.

The Whistle

My father stood on a street corner in Times Square whistling for me. When a cop asked him what he was doing, he said his son was a runaway and would come if he heard the whistle. My father stood there whistling for four days, but I hadn't gone to New York as I had hinted to my classmates; I stayed in Boston.

The Sunday afternoon I left home I got no further than the Hotel Touraine at the corner of Boylston and Tremont Street. I didn't have a destination in mind when I left. I didn't have a plan. I acted on the moment. The Touraine was a low-priced downtown hotel with lots of servicemen going in and out. I hoped I would not attract attention, went up to the desk, and paid cash for the room.

The first few days I walked around Chinatown and the waterfront. One night a couple of sailors in the hotel elevator asked me where to go for a beer and took me along as they headed for nearby joints. The girls they picked up saw that I was a kid, with only a little fuzz on my upper lip, flirted with me playfully, and left with the sailors. I went back the next night and through the window saw the same girls at a table with other guys. One of the girls spotted me and brought me in to join them. The girls adopted me as a sort of mascot. The guys they were with realized the girls liked me and treated me as if I were one of them. The girls always left with the guys; I headed back zombie-like, to the hotel. I got to know the girls and their territory, the dives and joints on Tremont Street and Columbus Avenue.

One night Shirley, who was older than the rest, sat me down with her in a booth and asked what was the matter. I shrugged her off. She left and came back later with an older guy whom she introduced as her friend, a waiter she used to work with at the Gay Nineties Café. Wallace C. Garden was short, my height, with slicked-down black hair and a moustache. He asked me what I was going to do when I ran out of money. I said I hadn't thought about it. He told me he could get me a job bussing tables and that I could stay with him at his mother's apartment in Bellingham Square, Chelsea. He said he was a homosexual but wouldn't bother me — he was diabetic and had troubles of his own.

I met him the next day at the Gay Nineties Café on Hayward Place; the manager said they needed a busboy and I could start that evening. I checked out of the Touraine and, accompanied by Wallace, took the trolley to Chelsea, where he told his mother I was a friend who would be staying for a while. She put me in a little room next to the kitchen. She had bad vision and made no fuss over me. I got the impression that I was not the first house guest her son had brought home. Wallace outfitted me with a spare pair of tuxedo trousers, suspenders, a white shirt and a bow tie, and we returned to Boston.

The Gay Nineties Café offered a stage show and singing waiters. I cleared the dishes. Occasionally, when Wallace wasn't feeling well, he asked me to put on his tuxedo jacket and wait on his tables. Each evening, Wallace collected a portion of the waiters' tips for me. My routine was going to bars in the afternoons, having a beer alongside the regulars, most of them drunks who lived in nearby rooming houses, and getting to know the girls. Shirley had "adopted" me and made sure I came to no harm. I was hoping for more, but the girls were little else than matronly towards me.

I may have run away from home but I hadn't gone far. I was less than a mile away and in familiar territory. My feelings were confused.

Instead of hanging around the corner with neighborhood kids, I had new friends. I was out from under my father's work demands and anger, but I was purposeless, aimless. I wondered about my mother and my little brother. Sometimes I ventured through the Boston Common and Public Garden to the Esplanade at the periphery of the West End, but no further.

In September the days turned shorter and colder. I knew I was missing school. One day late in the month Wallace motioned me into the waiters' locker room where he pointed to an article in that evening's Boston Globe about a mother's plea for help in finding her lost boy, with a picture of me. At that moment the manager came in with a policeman who asked me if I was the boy in the photo. I said I was. He took me to the Precinct Three police station on Joy Street and put me into a cell in the basement while the desk sergeant called my father. The sergeant told me I had a choice: go home with my father or stay in the cell. I told him I'd go home with my father.

Encouraging Developments

Once home, it seemed as if I had never left, as if I had only been away at summer camp. My six-year old brother, Joey, hugged me. My mother brought out lasagna and meatballs. My father stayed in the background. My mother told me later that she and my father had agreed he should ease up on me. Though I was only a mile from the Gay Nineties Café and the Tremont Street bars, I was in a different universe. I put away my clothes and slept in my own bed. I felt comfortable and secure at home.

The next day we were visited by Bill Gilligan, an athletic coach at Boston College who counseled truants as a volunteer youth worker for the Catholic Charitable Bureau.

I was cleared to return to school after an evaluation at the Judge Baker Guidance Center. Latin School Headmaster Joseph L. Powers suggested I transfer to English High School because I had missed too many classes. My grades were good and I could have caught up if I applied myself, but

I was uncomfortable with the thought of rejoining my class, so I agreed to the transfer.

Boston Latin School, on Avenue Louis Pasteur, was an imposing building in a prestigious location near the Fens, a block from Harvard Medical School, the Isabella Stuart Gardner Museum, the Museum of Fine Arts, and Boston's finest hospitals. By contrast, English High School, on Warren Avenue in the South End, was a relic of the previous century, with turrets and chimneys, and windows that didn't work, in a decrepit neighborhood filled with rooming houses and barrooms.

My first day at English High School proved eventful. In the morning, I stored my lunch bag in the basement locker assigned me. When I opened it at lunchtime there was a hole in it. Classmates said it was the mice. I teamed up with Al D'Amico and recruited home room captains in a petition drive to get an exterminator. Headmaster Walter F. Downey immediately agreed and word spread around the school that D'Amico and Del Vecchio got rid of the rats.

An even greater contrast between the two schools than the buildings and neighborhoods was their teaching methods. At Latin School scholarship was the standard, the method was discipline. At English High effort was the standard, the method, encouragement; to which I responded.

Bill Gilligan's next step in my salvation was to recommend me for the Boston Rotary Club's youth mentoring initiative. Each week I joined a different table of Rotarians at their luncheon meetings in the Hotel Statler. The Rotarians were an earnest and positive group who took a genuine interest in me and my future. The speakers gave testimonials to effort and determination. The men at the tables assured me that if I concentrated on my studies I would succeed. My pass to leave school every Wednesday for these luncheons earned me celebrity status at English High.

ONE DAY JOE Kozol, the smartest kid in the class — "*Kozol Knows All*" — said the Chess Club had an emergency: they were one player short for a match with Brookline High School. He asked me to fill in.

I told him I hadn't played for a couple of years, but was willing to do it. Overestimating my ability, Kozol placed me high on the team list, matching me against a top player on the other side. When my opponent opened a notebook in which to record each move, I feared he would dispatch me quickly. His opening gambit confirmed my fears, leading me to a desperate stratagem — to appear to be even more inept than I was. I slowed my play. When I pondered too long over an obvious response he impatiently said, "*Your* move." My plan was working. By this time the other boards had cleared — every member of our team had been defeated. The players clustered around us. I rapidly made a few reckless moves allowing my opponent to decimate my pieces and lulling him into a hasty anticlimactic move that trapped my king with nowhere to go but into check, gaining me a stalemate. He was stunned. We split the point. Final score: Brookline High School 12 ½, English High School ½. My reputation at school was secured.

Nothing much changed in the neighborhood after my return. I again was a benchwarmer with Ben Tankle at the Storrows' basketball games, and stopped by Charlie Maccarone's store after school to play the pinball machine. "How 'ya doing?" was the most penetrating question asked. The only change was that girls took more notice of me.

One afternoon as I was doing homework at the West End Branch Library, I became aware of a dark haired girl looking at me over the pages of a book. She glanced away when I saw her, but after a while joined me at the library table. Gina knew about me, and was intensely interested in why I left home. I told her my story. She told me hers. She lived alone with her father only a few doors from us on Chambers Street. Her mother was institutionalized; her older brother had married and moved out. She was two years older than me, dedicated to her religion, and lonely. She kept house for her father, attended mass each morning, and took the train every weekend to visit her institutionalized mother. She attached herself to me. We took long walks along the Esplanade arguing intently about religion. I challenged her beliefs which she tenaciously defended even as she gave in to my demands.

BILL GILLIGAN'S THIRD step in my salvation was getting me a job as a stage hand at the Boston College Summer School of Expressional Arts. I was sixteen. He arranged a ride for me with Leonard Nimoy, an acting student in the program, who lived in the next block on Chambers Street. Each morning, Lenny picked me up in his old Plymouth for the drive to the Newton campus. He had begun acting at the Elizabeth Peabody Settlement House and had a definite plan — when he finished the B.C. summer program he was going to California to study at the Pasadena Playhouse. While I hammered together stage scenery, Lenny's deep voice and stage presence landed him featured roles.

The summer drama program was a haven for homosexual student priests but I never had a problem; these young scholastics were gentle, caring, and devout. After my experiences as a runaway I knew how to rebuff any advances. The days went quickly. I learned a lot about acting and theater.

MY SENIOR YEAR at English High School started out positively. Al D'Amico asked me to be his running mate in his campaign for 1950 class president. Our posters showed D'Amico and Del Vecchio stomping on rats. We won.

When my English teacher, Mr. Eccles, asked me about my college plans I told him I didn't have any. On his advice I applied for a Navy ROTC scholarship, which would provide tuition and a $50 monthly allowance in return for service as a Navy officer on graduation. I won the scholarship and was accepted in the Tufts College NROTC program.

The English High School basketball team won the Boston Conference, putting it into the Tech Tourney finals at the Boston Garden for the first time. I wasn't a cheerleader but the squad asked me to lead the cheering at the game. Our team made up a big deficit, nearly nipping the favored Attleboro at the end.

At graduation I delivered the class oration, closing with Browning's *"...a man's reach should exceed his grasp, or what's a heaven for?"* My entire family showed up. The lost summer of 1948 was a distant memory.

CHAPTER 6

PRINCIPLES OF FLIGHT

Dramatis Personae

The personnel of the Tufts College NROTC unit faced a challenge: how to mold students in a permissive college environment into naval officers. They received little support from the faculty, who did not regard Naval Engineering or Navigation bona fide academic subjects. The Naval Science classes were not even held on the main campus, which was dominated by departmental fiefdoms, each in its own ivy-covered edifice. The unit occupied a nondescript building on a commercial street at the edge of the campus.

On the tree-covered hill looking down on the NROTC building, professors wore tweeds, smoked pipes, and interacted with students. In the NROTC unit, officers wore uniforms, returned salutes, and did their best to establish a military routine. Midshipman uniforms were required dress for the weekly drills, students conformed to military protocols, stood when the instructors entered the classrooms and addressed them as "*Sir.*" The atmosphere was not complicated by the presence of females, for these were the only classrooms in the college without women.

The Korean War changed campus attitudes about the NROTC unit. On June 25, 1950, five years after the end of World War II, the communist North Korean army crossed the 38th parallel, invading U.S. ally South Korea. President Truman ordered intervention, and within two weeks the U.S. military had suffered seven thousand dead, wounded or captured. By August, U.S. forces had been pushed to Pusan where, with their backs to the Sea of Japan, they made a stand. A successful U.S. amphibious assault at Inchon on September 15 seemed to be a turning point, but when Chinese forces crossed the Yalu River in November the prospects appeared grim. The Tufts naval contingent took on new importance.

At NROTC orientation I met Rick Breitenfeld, an engineering student from New Rochelle, New York. Rick gave me the college tour, introduced me to his fellow thespians at the Tufts Arena Stage, and to Dick Goodwin, his best friend in the dorm. He said that with my theater experience I should try out for the college drama club. I got a small part in the opening play, qualifying me to be a member of Pen, Paint and Pretzels, "3P's." The Arena Stage building became my frequent destination after class, and a second home, for I was an "off-campus" student, commuting daily by trolley from the West End to the Medford campus. After rehearsals, Rick entertained cast and crew with show tunes on the piano, and we ate pizza and drank wine in front of the fire.

My parents told me to bring my friends home for a "good Italian meal." They hosted many a contingent from 3P's for Sunday dinner, which delighted my father, for he had a new captive audience for his jokes. Rick reciprocated by inviting me to his home for the Thanksgiving holiday. His was the first single-family house that I had been in; everyone in my neighborhood lived in a rental walk-up flat. His parents warmly welcomed me into their home. There was a grand piano in a living room lined with bookcases. His father was an engineer and patent attorney, his mother an officer of the New York Ethical Culture Society. I felt as comfortable with Rick's parents as he did with mine.

Dick Goodwin, Rick's friend at the dorm, was a fearsome presence on the campus — at the top of his class and the editor of the Tufts Weekly. Dick confided that he had a problem at the newspaper: none of his reporters was funny and the writing was predictable and repetitious. Dick had been exposed to my father's comic repertoire and thought I might be able to help out. He suggested a sports column.

I consulted with my uncle Sal, the gambler, who said he would ask his bookmaker for inside dope on the ponies at Suffolk Downs. Sal passed along some Damon Runyon paddock talk about the track, which I put in a column titled "Straight from the Horse's Mouth," by "*Mr. Z.*" Goodwin printed it!

Sal told me later that his source was his old dentist, "Doc" Sagansky, a Tufts Dental School graduate who in the 20's saw patients at his dental office in Scollay Square, one of whom was Sal. Sagansky got into the numbers racket, a more lucrative enterprise than pulling teeth. When Sal contacted him with my request, Sagansky obliged, considering the info was for Sal's nephew, a Tufts student from the West End.

Dick's next sports gambit was to outfit us with official looking identification cards imprinted "PRESS — TUFTS WEEKLY." Our first destination was Fenway Park. Dick parked on Lansdowne Street, and we confidently approached the Press entrance where we flashed our "PRESS" passes and were waved through the turnstiles. I learned the power of the press.

The Time of Your Life

I was one of sixty midshipmen manning the rails of the converted destroyer escort USS Carpellotti (APD-136) as we steamed out into Hampton Roads from the Norfolk Navy Base on an early June morning in 1951. The captain's orders were to make sailors out of us.

First year midshipmen are at the bottom of the ship's ladder, assigned to clean toilets, swab decks, polish the brass. Nothing they attempt is accepted the first time. The lowliest seaman can order them to redo any task. Our first assignment was to clean the heads.

The ship steered a northeast course for Newfoundland, where it joined a task group led by the battleship Missouri (BB-63) for a North Atlantic crossing. Soon after rendezvous we came alongside the Missouri to transfer mail to it via ship-to-ship lines. The battleship dwarfed our vessel, displacing 45,000 tons to the Carpellotti's 1,450. Its three turrets housed nine 16" guns; our ship had a single 5" turret. During the transfer I spotted a midshipman jumping up and down at the Missouri's rail, wildly waving his arms in my direction. It was my classmate Rick Breitenfeld, who had drawn the Missouri for his first cruise.

As we entered the northern latitudes about ten degrees south of the Arctic Circle on a course for the Shetland Islands, the clouds lowered, the sea turned from green to gray, and the wind began churning up whitecaps on the swells. Orders came to secure the ship for heavy weather, dog the hatches, and stow all loose gear. I was on the bridge for the midwatch when a North Atlantic storm engulfed the task group. Waves higher than the superstructure caused the ship to broach and twist. Certain that we would capsize, I wedged myself into a corner and held on.

At the end of my watch I made my way down the ship's ladders to the midshipmen's quarters, to find a scene of misery in a compartment filled with the odor of diesel fuel and retching. The perspective from the bridge, though frightening, had spared me from the sailor's curse of seasickness. Below decks I soon joined my shipmates in despair. I told a couple of buddies, Naval Academy midshipmen, that it was better topside. We ignored the orders to stay below and opened a hatch to the outside, where the cold rain relieved our nausea. We decided not to throw ourselves into the sea.

We anchored in Edinburgh and hit the bars, where we told the girls about our dramatic crossing, omitting the embarrassing personal details. Our sea stories improved at each successive anchorage: Bergen, Malmo, Copenhagen. By Lisbon, our last liberty port, we had perfected our routine. Our return over southern waters was smooth. The last port on the cruise was Guantanamo Bay Naval Base, where Rick and I met up at the Officers Club pool, ordered Anejo punch, downed Hatuey beer, and traded stories with the midshipmen from other ships in the task group. By the time we debarked at the Norfolk Navy Base we had become sailors.

THE SUMMER WAS over and I was back at Tufts. Still active in the theater group I tried out for the role of Joe, the lead character in William Saroyan's "The Time of Your Life."

Saroyan's play compressed the foibles of the world into a small fantasy played out in a bar on the San Francisco waterfront. There is no evident plot. Joe occupies a table at center stage and interacts with the characters who float in and out: Kitty Duval, the prostitute with a heart of gold; the Arab, a harmless eccentric; Kit Carson, an old Indian fighter with fantastic tales; Nick, the philosophical bartender; Blick, an evil cop who bullies the vulnerable denizens of the bar. For me, this was familiar territory. I knew these characters. Kitty Duval was Shirley, the girl in the Tremont Street bars who adopted me when I was a runaway; Blick was the mean cop in the Precinct 3 Police Station; Kit Carson was my uncle Sal, full of fabulous stories. I got the part. They cast Rick as Kit Carson. I was having the time of my life.

WHILE MY CLASSMATES and I were training as midshipmen, U.S ground forces were engaged in a bloody land battle on the Korean peninsula. Unlike World War II, where the stakes were obvious, the Korean War was confusing. Although Americans accepted as obligatory that the U.S. defend its South Korean allies when North Korean forces crossed the 38th parallel in June 1950, they were not prepared for a protracted war with a distant enemy that posed no direct threat to U.S. territory. The major political issue was how to extricate the country from this unpopular U.N. "Police Action." President Truman understood the public sentiment. When General MacArthur maneuvered to escalate the conflict, Truman relieved him of his command. Even though the opposing forces were at a stalemate at the 38th parallel, fighting a useless war of attrition, it was not until two years later, with the cease-fire of July 27, 1953, that the "forgotten war" in Korea ended.

Public concern had shifted to Cold War hysteria about domestic enemies. Wisconsin Senator Joseph McCarthy, and the House Un-American Activities Committee, made political capital out of fears about a Soviet atom bomb threat, Russian dominance in Eastern Europe, and the fall of China to communism. They led a witch hunt against communists in the State Department, Hollywood, and universities.

Our midshipman unit, meanwhile, received training in amphibious warfare at the Little Creek, Virginia, Marine detachment, aviation at the Corpus Christi Naval Air Station, and celestial navigation aboard the heavy cruiser USS Albany (CA-123). On my last North Atlantic cruise I was able to visit London, Paris and Barcelona on liberty. I applied for the highly competitive Naval Aviation training as my active duty preference.

In my senior year I was elected to Phi Beta Kappa, but the best news was a letter from the Bureau of Naval Personnel informing me that I had been accepted for Naval Aviation training. On graduation in June, 1954, I was commissioned Ensign, United States Navy, and immediately ordered to active duty with Fleet Aircraft Service Repair Squadron 121 (FASRON 121), at the Naval Auxiliary Air Station, Chincoteague, Virginia.

Principles of Flight

FASRON 121's mission was to service aircraft within 48 hours of deplaning at a CB-constructed remote landing strip. The drill was organization and speed. After three months of routine squadron duties my orders arrived to report to the Naval Air Training Command, Pensacola, Florida. I headed south out of Chincoteague as Hurricane Carol skirted us heading north.

The September, 1954, entering Pre-Flight class at Forrest Sherman Field was a confident group of recent Naval Academy and NROTC grads. We bunked at the Bachelor Officer Quarters, received snappy salutes from enlisted personnel, and were served dinner in the Officers Mess by Filipino stewards in starched whites. When I sat down for dinner the first night there was an intense discussion underway at the opposite end of the table. The young officer holding court was arguing that if you don't use power you lose it; that the U.S. should use its might to roll back Soviet puppet regimes in Eastern Europe. I asked my neighbors who this Cold War gladiator was. They informed me he was Donald Rumsfeld, a champion wrestler from Princeton. I couldn't resist engaging him — my debating instincts had been aroused — and asked my table mates if they were up for some fun. They were, and we launched into a discussion about containment and how militarism once unleashed couldn't be reined in. Rumsfeld took the bait at first, but soon caught on to our tactics and shifted to gamesmanship and humor, a scene that played out with variations nearly every night. When orientation ended and we were assigned to outlying fields, Rumsfeld and I parted as if we had been war buddies.

THE BLACKBOARD IN the Whiting Field hangar listed "Weir" as the instructor, "Del Vecchio" the student, for Flight A-1, the first basic training flight. I had prepared by studying the Pilot's Handbook and the aircraft manual, and sitting for hours in an SNJ cockpit until I could instinctively locate every instrument and flight control. I felt ready. Awaiting me was my instructor, Lt. Tom Weir, even shorter than my five feet six inches. He dispensed with the pre-flight briefing, and as we headed for the flight line said "Your Ground School record is good. From here on, concentrate on what I do and don't be afraid to ask questions."

Lt. Weir led me around the aircraft through the pre-flight inspection, then told me to strap into the forward cockpit. Standing on the wing next to me he had me close my eyes and rapid-fire asked me to touch each flight control and cockpit instrument as he reeled them off: "wobble pump; gear lever; flaps; fuel tank selector switch: left, right, reserve; primer; hand hydraulic pump; rudder trim; elevator trim; carburetor heat; prop pitch; fuel mixture; battery switch; starter switch; mags; manifold pressure gauge; oil temperature gauge; turn and bank indicator; altimeter; air speed indicator; rate of climb indicator; cylinder head temperature gauge; clock; radio; canopy latch." My preparation paid off. He nodded O.K., then talked me through the start procedure: "fuel mixture rich; prop low pitch; fuel lever to reserve tank; prime four strokes; battery switch on; magneto on; hold starter switch up to start, then throttle back to 600 to 800 rpms; check oil pressure for 40 psi minimum; prop pitch to full increase; test flight controls: stick, ailerons, rudder; hold brakes." Then he climbed into the rear cockpit, said over the intercom "I've got it; take your feet off the rudder pedals," called for taxi clearance, gave the crewman the signal to remove chocks, gunned the engine to get the aircraft moving, and taxied out.

I was going through the same training routine World War II pilots had received ten years before. North American Aviation's rugged T-6 "Texan" was the primary trainer for the Air Force, the "SNJ" for the Navy — the difference being the yellow paint job and a tailhook in the Navy version. British, Canadian and Australian pilots flew it as the "Harvard" before reporting to Hurricane and Spitfire squadrons. Outfitted with guns and bomb racks, the T-6 was still in use by air forces around the world. In Korea, the U.S. used it as a spotter.

The SNJ was powered by a Pratt & Whitney R-1340 radial engine producing 550 horsepower, had a maximum speed of 200 knots, a cruising speed of 130 knots, and a range of 700 nautical miles. A sliding "birdcage" canopy enclosed its tandem cockpit, where the student pilot sat in the forward seat and the instructor in the rear. The high nose in the aircraft's three-point attitude obscured the pilot's forward vision while taxiing, requiring use of the rudders to fishtail the aircraft in an "S" pattern for visibility.

Lt. Weir held short of the duty runway until receiving clearance to take off, then taxied onto the centerline, describing the procedure as he carried it out: "Throttle forward to the stop: 36 inches manifold pressure, 2250 rpm; release brakes; as forward airspeed increases engine torque pulls the nose to the left — correct with right rudder; as the aircraft accelerates ease the stick forward to take-off attitude and the aircraft becomes airborne. Climb at 95 knots, 1950 rpm, 30" manifold pressure. At 100 feet raise wheels then flaps, and make a turn away from the field. At 1000 feet switch fuel from reserve tank to left tank and wobble pump a few strokes to ensure an uninterrupted fuel flow." He leveled off at

5000 feet, 130 knots, trimmed, and turned the controls over to me, with instructions to maintain altitude, airspeed and heading.

The secret to learning aircraft control is to isolate the variables. Power is used to maintain a constant airspeed and trim to maintain level flight. Lt. Weir's method of instruction was to build confidence. His object was success in small increments. I thought I was doing O.K. when he abruptly shook the stick and took the controls saying "I've got it; check three o'clock." Off our starboard wing, bright yellow against the blue sky, was a SNJ a couple of hundred yards away, on a heading angling towards us, at the same altitude and closing. I had been oblivious to what was going on around us, with my head in the cockpit. Lt. Weir added power and banked sharply away, admonishing me: "Lesson number one — keep your head on a swivel." Then he talked me through a series of climbs and descents, following which he had me combine the two. After several of these maneuvers, as the sweat was pouring into my flight goggles, Lt. Weir shook the stick and said, "I have the controls; enough for today," and headed back to Whiting Field. After the aircraft was chocked, Lt. Weir said: "Good job. Read up on landings; you'll be doing those tomorrow."

Some of the theories taught at Ground School were demonstrated in simulators: hypoxia in the low-pressure chamber, escape from a ditched airplane in the Dilbert Dunker; but actual time aloft was required to learn the principles of flight; theory alone was inadequate.

Hypoxia is caused by a lack of oxygen, a condition that results in light-headedness, disorientation, and unconsciousness. At altitudes above 10,000 feet in an unpressurized aircraft such as the SNJ these symptoms begin, usually unrecognized by the pilot. War movies are full of scenes where the pilot blacks out and regains consciousness just in time to pull out of a spin. In Ground School, students sit facing each other in a low pressure chamber as a pump evacuates the air, simulating an aircraft climbing to altitude. A rubber balloon hanging from a string expands as the pressure of the air entrapped in the balloon exceeds the pressure in the chamber — visual evidence of the unseen and unfelt loss of air. The instructor, wearing an oxygen mask, tells the students through an intercom hookup to perform rudimentary tasks such as counting on their fingers, keeping hands outstretched, touching one's nose. One by one the students become disoriented and fail these tasks. When someone drifts off the instructor helps him put on his oxygen mask and he observes his comrades. Not until then does the student appreciate the extent to which his faculties were compromised by lack of oxygen.

The Dilbert Dunker simulates a ditching at sea, where the aircraft noses over and the pilot finds himself underwater, strapped into the cockpit and upside down. The device is a cockpit section mounted on tracks angled at 45 degrees at the end of the pool. The student straps into the contraption. When the instructor pulls the lever the cockpit plunges into the pool and inverts. The instructions are to unbuckle the seat belt and push *down* to clear the fuselage, then swim for the surface. This runs counter to one's instincts; when underwater you want to swim *up*.

When a World War II Hellcat or Bearcat returned from combat with flight controls shot up, the pilot could ditch his propeller driven craft at low speed alongside the carrier with a good chance of surviving. In Korea, F9F Panthers and F2H Banshee jet fighters had to ditch at higher speeds. If the aircraft didn't break up on impact, its heavier weight caused it to sink rapidly, with little time for the pilot to unbuckle and swim clear. A better alternative than ditching at sea was required. The solid propellant Martin-Baker ejection seat was the answer. A race was on to improve it so it would work at low altitudes, so important for emergencies while taking off or landing on a carrier. The hope was that ditching at sea would go the way of the Spad.

Nonetheless, the Navy required its student pilots to survive the Dilbert Dunker. There was lots of flying to be done, including carrier qualifications, before a student would be at the controls of a fighter equipped with an ejection seat. Moreover, the Navy still had prop aircraft in the fleet, including the workhorse Douglas A-1 Skyraider, a single-engine attack aircraft that was a carrier mainstay for ground support.

The Principles of Flight doctrine as taught in Ground School attributed lift to the shape of the wing, explained by the Bernoulli principle that air flowing *over* an airfoil's curved upper surface is reduced in pressure due to the greater distance it travels than the air passing *under* the wind. Because of this pressure differential, the greater pressure on the bottom *lifts* the wing. The theory is illustrated by the Venturi effect: as a fluid or gas is forced through a narrowed opening it accelerates and its pressure falls.

I had doubts about this explanation. The balsa wood airplanes I launched by hand from the top of the hill in the Boston Common had flat wings and flew perfectly well, as did the paper airplanes I tossed out of my window at 75 Chambers Street that flew over the roof of St. Joseph's Church. But Ground School was no time to be waving my hand in class acting smart.

I prepared for the next day of instruction with Lt. Weir by concentrating on the landing procedures spelled out in the Pilot's Handbook. I was not worrying about Bernoulli or Venturi.

Murphy's Law

"What can go wrong will go wrong."

Under Lt. Weir's tutelage I passed my check ride, soloed, and began logging first pilot time on proficiency flights. One late afternoon, while practicing stalls and spins in a cloudless sky over Whiting Field, I suddenly realized that all my ground reference points had disappeared. Smoke from brush fires was obscuring the landmarks I used to navigate to and from the field. I had a brief moment of panic, but quickly hit upon a way to reorient myself. I would fly due south until reaching Pensacola Bay, which should be free of brush fire smoke because of the onshore winds from the Gulf, and then find my way back to Whiting by following Route 87 north. I checked my fuel, which was ample, and took up a southerly heading.

I was confident I would be able to navigate because of the distinctive features of the Pensacola Bay area. Ten miles south of Whiting Field, Blackwater Bay defines the east side of a peninsula that is bounded on the west by Escambia Bay. The tip of the peninsula points to Pensacola Beach, a distinctive narrow strip of sand. At a cruising speed of 130 knots I would be over the inlets in about five minutes, and should be able to see the larger bays in about ten because the smoke from brush fires would be dissipating due to southerly winds. But instead of blue water and familiar beaches all I could see was low-lying smoke alternately obscuring and revealing green vegetation. After twenty minutes on a course that should have brought me to the edge of the Gulf of Mexico I was still over land. As I was pondering my next move, which would be a humiliating radio transmission giving my call sign and announcing that I was lost, I spotted alternating white and green flashes of light below. This was a reassuring development. It had to be an airport rotating beacon. When visibility deteriorates to less than three miles or cloud cover lowers to under a thousand feet, airfields activate beacons to aid airmen. I throttled back, descended to a thousand feet, headed towards the flashing light penetrating the haze, and shortly crossed over the boundary of a large airfield complex. I didn't attempt radio contact since the SNJ was equipped only with a VHF transmitter, and I didn't know the airfield or the tower frequency. My only option was to enter the traffic pattern and hope for the best. The windsock at the center of the field indicated light westerly surface winds, so I throttled back to 90 knots, descended to 500 feet, dropped the landing gear and entered the downwind leg, setting up for a landing on runway 30.

Although I didn't have radio contact, my intentions were obvious. The tower flashed a steady green light clearing me to land. I banked left, placed flaps at twenty degrees, and descended at 80 knots, making a three-point touchdown at midfield. I taxied rapidly off the runway and headed for the tower, where a huge "EGLIN AFB" sign was over the entrance. An Air Force ground crewman waved me into a parking spot next to a F-86 Sabre jet. I shut down the engine, climbed out, and walked into the tower building fearing a reckoning.

The Operations personnel paid little attention to me. They were clustered around a pilot at the far end of the counter. I told the airman who came over to me that Whiting was my home field, that I had become disoriented in the haze, and needed a heading back. He said, "Three two zero degrees, twenty miles, tell me when you're ready to go," and returned to the other end of the counter. I went over, curious about the attraction. In the center of the group was a short, dark-skinned pilot with an unlit cigar in his teeth bantering with the men. His name patch read "Maj. Jabara." Every student pilot knew who Major James Jabara was. He was the first U.S. jet ace, credited with fifteen kills in Korea. My problem was that I couldn't tell the story of my landing at Eglin and seeing Jabara, for that would reveal my embarrassing lost odyssey over the Pensacola hinterlands.

I motioned to the airman that I was ready to go. After starting the SNJ, I got a flashing green light from the tower to taxi followed by a steady green for takeoff. I leveled off at 1000 feet, maintaining a heading of 300 degrees to correct for a westerly wind. The visibility was worsening as the lowering angle of the afternoon sun gave a reddish-brown tint to the smoke, but luckily I intercepted Route 87 near the Santa Rosa auxiliary field and followed it to Whiting Field, where I entered the landing pattern uneventfully. The only evidence of my unplanned excursion that day was my flight log book entry showing *two* landings.

Carrier Qualifications

By the time I progressed to Carrier Qualifications, the last phase of Basic Training, my entering flight school class had been seriously thinned out as predicted. The commanding officer's opening words to us our first day at Forrest Sherman Field had been: "Look to your right, then to your left. Only one of you will finish the program." This was proving true.

Flying aptitude manifests itself early. An instructor can usually gauge within the first few flights if a student is pilot material. Whiting Field was not only the first, but also the last flying experience for many aspiring naval aviators. "Downs" (unsatisfactory training flights), were commonplace, and if the student didn't improve on a check ride with a different instructor he was dropped immediately. Rather than waiting to be washed out, many simply gave up and dropped out on their own request (DOR). An eager young officer might have passed the aptitude exam and possessed an outstanding academic record, but not until he was at the controls would his flying ability be put to the test. The looks we made to our right and to our left at opening assembly gave no clue as to who would make it and who wouldn't. Some unlikely candidates did and some of the most impressive didn't.

The aim of the first phase of basic was to build student confidence. Instructors like Lt. Weir were mentors. Successive stages: Aerobatics, Formation Flying, Gunnery, Bombing, were designed to develop proficiency. Expectations increased and instructors became progressively more demanding. Only in combat, however, would the ultimate goal of Naval Aviation training — the pilot's mastery of his environment — be proved, but there were indications along the way, such as how a student handled emergencies, and carrier landings. I felt I was ready for the carrier. I had already logged 160 hours in the air, half of it as first pilot, and had made 170 landings. At the controls of the now familiar SNJ I experienced the fighter pilot's high: the phenomenon that one is so integrated with the aircraft it feels as if it is an extension of your body.

The CarQual instructor briefed our group of six student pilots in the Barin Field ready room. He said he expected every one of us to qualify; we knew how to land and would only have to factor in the assistance of the Landing Signal Officer (LSO). He would be the LSO for our carrier landing practice at the field, and aboard the carrier the day of qualifications. He explained that landing on the carrier should be no more difficult than landing on a runway, and in some respects would be easier because there would be fewer variables. We would not be confronted with a pitching carrier deck in heavy seas, a situation that can cause the most seasoned pilot's knuckles to whiten as he grips the stick on final approach. Our carrier would be in the calm waters of the Gulf, within twenty miles of the coast. There would be no crosswinds to deal with since the wind would be directly down the deck, and touchdown would be at a lower relative speed than on a runway because the carrier's forward speed adds to that of the surface wind. [When "recovering" aircraft, a carrier turns to head directly into the wind. Steaming at twenty knots into a ten knot wind the effective wind speed down the deck is thirty knots. At a landing airspeed of 75 knots the relative speed of the SNJ over the carrier deck at touchdown would be only 45 knots.] Lastly, we would have the benefit of the Landing Signal Officer to guide us to the spot on the deck where the SNJ tailhook would catch an arresting wire.

We had two weeks to practice before our scheduled fly out to the USS Saipan, (CVL-48), a straight deck light carrier that had seen Korean War service. The instructor divided the group into three sections, each composed of a leader and a wingman, and told us to get airborne. He would talk us through the carrier landing pattern from a position at the approach end of the runway. We joined in formation and entered the *upwind* leg of the field landing pattern, (heading *into* the wind parallel to the runway). On the upwind leg the group formed an echelon with each aircraft to the right and stepped down from the aircraft ahead. On the instructor's radio command the division leader passed the lead to his wingman with a jerk of his head to the left while simultaneously patting his helmet, broke left for a 180 degree turn to the *downwind* leg, (*with* the wind), and dropped gear, flaps and tailhook in preparation for landing. At a count of five, to ensure distance separation, the next aircraft in sequence broke left and entered the downwind leg. These maneuvers resulted in a column of six SNJ's heading downwind, with the runway off their left wingtips, ready to make the landing approach. At the *initial*, a point abeam the intended touchdown point, the student turned left for the final approach to the runway centerline. The LSO awaited him, ready to pick him up visually on final descent and guide him onto the deck.

The Landing Signal Officer was the key man on an aircraft carrier recovering aircraft after a mission, particularly on a pitching deck in heavy weather and especially when a returning pilot had mechanical trouble. The LSO's role was part pilot and part pantomime — virtually the second man in the cockpit. He wore distinctive attire: Reflective tape outlined the arms and legs of his flight suit; in each hand he grasped a tennis racket-sized paddle strung with strips of reflective tape; on his head a baseball cap, eyes shaded by Ray Ban sunglasses; at his feet was a Very pistol loaded with a red flare ready to be fired for a waveoff. As the pilot entered the final approach the LSO took control of the landing using paddles and body English. High paddles meant you're too high, a lean to the left or to the right meant you are off centerline in the direction of the lean; low paddles — too low, bring it up. A furious criss-crossing of the paddles over the head meant WAVE OFF: add full throttle, get the nose up and bank left away from the carrier's island structure. These basic moves were accentuated by a repertoire of gyrations tailored to the situation, such as exaggerated leans left or right. If the pilot succeeded in staying on glide path, centerline, airspeed, and aircraft attitude, as the aircraft passed over the edge of the fantail the LSO drew a paddle across his throat in an engine "Cut" signal, and unless the approach was spoiled by a last minute bounce, the aircraft caught an arresting wire that brought it to an abrupt but welcome stop.

We got to know our instructor LSO and he got to know us. On the day of the fly out we taxied out as a group, joined in formation, the instructor in the lead, and headed south. Shortly after crossing the beach we spotted the Saipan as it was turning into the wind. The instructor passed the lead to his wingman and broke away to land first and position himself at the fantail as LSO. After he made radio contact with the flight and cleared us to land, we performed as we had practiced at the field: formed into echelon, broke left successively, configured our aircraft for landing, and followed his signals to touchdown. The flight did well. All students qualified with six landings each, after which we circled in formation until he joined up to lead the flight back to Barin Field. After we landed, a sailor with a Speed Graphic camera photographed each of us posed next to an SNJ, for our hometown newspapers. My logbook that day bore the stamped entry: "Qualified this date in carrier landing. Made *six* landings aboard the USS SAIPAN."

"June 06, 1955, NAAS Barin Field, Foley, Ala., standing by an SNJ after completing Carrier Qualifications is Del Vecchio, F. V." (Official U.S. Navy photo.)

Shooting Star

My orders directed me to report to Naval Air Station Memphis for jet training. I would be flying the TV-2, a Lockheed F-80 "Shooting Star" interceptor stretched by three feet to accommodate a dual cockpit. After presenting my orders to the Officer of the Day I dropped off my gear in a room at Bachelor Officers Quarters and headed to the flight line for a look.

Only eight years separated the development of the F-80 from the T-6 "Texan"/SNJ. Though comparable in size to the T-6, the F-80 was as different as a Bugatti to a Model T. Each was a testament to American initiative and ingenuity.

North American Aviation began development of the T-6 in 1935 without any commitments; it performed so well it was quickly purchased by the U.S. Army Air Corps as its primary trainer. This rugged prop aircraft trained more Allied pilots than any other.

Lockheed secretly developed the Shooting Star in a matter of months in 1943 in a furious race to put a jet fighter into the air to challenge the Messerschmitt Me262 "Swallow." Jet-powered Me262's had begun to decimate Allied bomber formations in late 1944 and early 1945, but due to mixed objectives from the Nazi hierarchy not enough were ready to prevent Wermacht surrender May 8, 1945.

Messerschmitt and Lockheed engineers on different continents operated in remarkable parallel. Their parent corporations: Messerschmitt AG, a joint stock company, and Lockheed, a California corporation, were the successors to aircraft manufacturers whose markets collapsed in the Great Depression, went bankrupt, but later reconstituted themselves as new military markets emerged for their products. The capitalists heading both companies understood how to exploit the politics and power of war; one side the aggressor, the other, defender. In isolation from each other, and in total secrecy, the engineers on both sides operated in much the same way: as innovators in teams unencumbered by technical or organizational convention.

German rearmament beginning in 1933 was the impetus for aircraft designer and political insider Willy Messerschmitt to gain control of Bavarian Aircraft Works and pioneer aircraft design for the Third Reich. He formed a team of engineers who created warplanes that blitzed the skies of Europe. One of their innovations was "*light-weight construction.*" The engineer's instinct, when a structural element fails, is to beef it up. In aircraft design, strengthening a structural member adds weight and has to be compensated for by greater engine power, which also increases weight. There is little or no gain in performance. Messerschmitt designed *down*, so that structural elements reinforce each other, resulting in lighter weight and higher performance. As more powerful engines were developed the result was increased *speed*, as was demonstrated by the Messerschmitt 109, the formidable interceptor he produced for the Luftwaffe.

In 1939 Messerschmitt set up Project P.1065, a secret effort dedicated to revolutionizing aircraft design with jet power. By 1943, the project had tested the Me262 Swallow interceptor and began manufacture. If it hadn't been for a confusion of strategic purpose and interference from the top that fragmented the products of Messerschmitt's team and delayed production, their work might have been decisive in the outcome of the war. This was not the case with the development of the "Shooting Star."

In early 1943, British intelligence uncovered the Me262 Swallow project. Top U. S. Army Air Force commanders consulted with Lockheed which, without a contract or a commitment, put together a team of twenty-eight engineers in a secret project dubbed "Skunk Works." ["*Skonk Works*" was a dilapidated factory on the outskirts of Dogpatch, the home of Lil Abner, the leading character in Al Capp's comic strip of the same name. The Skonk Works is where Big Barnsmell and his cousin Barney ground dead skunks and old shoes into a putrid concoction in an old still. The odor permeating the vicinity guaranteed there would be no intruders.]

The Skunk Works operated much like Messerschmitt's Project P.1065, but with a major difference. There was no confusion of purpose on the part of the Americans, and no meddling from higher ups. The Army High Command was focused on one objective: a jet fighter that could outfly the Me262. The race to catch up was on.

The engineers at the Skunk Works employed a similar aircraft design philosophy as their counterparts in Project P.1065: simplify; *design down*. The challenge was to create a rugged but lightweight airframe to be powered by the British deHavilland "Goblin" turbojet engine. How could the aluminum airframe be simultaneously lightened, strengthened, and streamlined?

The Lockheed engineers had an advantage over the German team, which started with an airframe to which engines were *added* in a pod under each wing, increasing weight and drag. The Lockheed engineers started with an engine *around* which they could create an airframe. They ingeniously solved the weight and strength challenge by inventing a method of bending and flush riveting the aluminum components of the airframe. The sleek "Shooting Star" airframe was the streamlined result. They solved the engineering challenges in only three months and completed a prototype only five months later, in November, 1943. Within a year they delivered a dozen pre-production models, but production was delayed by a test flight crash caused by an engine fire. It was not until two months after Germany's surrender that the first operational aircraft were put into service.

In 1947 the Shooting Star set a world speed record, and in the first jet versus jet aerial battle, shot down a MiG-15 in Korea in 1950. I would soon be at its controls.

Beale Street

"'Del Vecchio', what's that, Italian? O.K. if I call you 'Del'?"

The questioner was Fred Lacey, 2nd Lt., USMC, beer in hand, cigar in mouth, sitting on the edge of my bunk in the Bachelor Officer Quarters, jawing with my roommate Sherwood Drake, 2nd Lt., USMC, lying in the opposite bunk.

"Sure," I said, "O.K. if I call you 'Ole Boy'?"

"Suits me fine," he said with a grin, "mostly they call me 'Lace'."

"Del, we'll introduce you to Beale Street tonight," said Drake, rising to shake my hand. "You'll have the weekend to recover."

Fred Lacey's sportive vernacular derived from his home town of Monroe, Louisiana. He had refined it at Ole Miss. Drake's poise, from a proper upbringing in a Virginia first family, concealed an adventurous disposition.

The Naval Air Station was located ten miles north of Memphis, in Millington, Tennessee. Beale Street, the "Home of the Blues," was a typical honky-tonk strip running from downtown Memphis to the Mississippi River. The only difference from Scollay Square or the bars on Tremont Street was the accents. Our civvies, and Lace's drawl fooled nobody; we were marks. We ordered beers in a couple of joints, then headed for West Memphis, ("Beale Street West"), located ten miles west across the Mississippi, in Arkansas. After cruising through a dilapidated downtown littered with crumby bars, Lace said, "Let's go to the Peabody." We retraced our route, and parked across from the Peabody, a fine old Memphis hotel. On our way to the bar I noticed a tripod in the lobby with a Playbill: "*Tryouts — The Twelve — Memphis Little Theatre — Rooftop Lounge — Saturday, 8 PM.*" I made a mental note to return the next night.

"The Twelve" was experimenting with improvisational theater. Barbara Cason, a Memphis native with a local television show and a compulsion to be an actress had seen the Compass Players in Chicago and thought their improvisational method could work in an area like Memphis, which had to rely on local talent. Classical theater and "method" acting involves years of professional study and dedication. Improvisation requires principally the courage to get up in front of an audience and wing it.

Barbara welcomed me eagerly. I told her I had done some acting in college, but would probably be leaving Memphis in less than two months as soon as I completed my jet training syllabus. She urged me to take part, saying she needed to build up the experience of the group of twelve students and residents she had recruited.

Improvisation lends itself to the abilities of those who take part. We began by sitting in a circle and answering Barbara's question: "What role do you see yourself playing?" When it came to me, I said: "A dreamer who sits in a bar and sticks up for the little guy." Of course I was talking about Joe in Saroyan's "The Time of Your Life." By the time we had gone around the circle we had a cast of characters. Barbara's next question was:

"What happens and what do you do?" People reacted differently, and to type. Some were assertive, some reactive. The product of this exercise was a scenario similar to Saroyan's: A few of us would sit at a bar, and interact as others came in. We had some success at the very outset, because everyone felt comfortable with the character he was portraying — usually himself.

Classical theater was at the other extreme. Actors were regimented. They delivered their memorized lines at fixed locations on the stage with formal intonation and structured movements and gestures. In Greek tragedy actors' faces were expressionless — concealed behind masks. "Method" acting, which dominated American theater at the time, employed a discipline of its own — basically Freudian. The actors were taught to burrow deeply into their subconscious experience and extract the emotion or mood the role required. Acting could be agony — *"One must suffer to be an actor."* Improvisation, in contrast, was fun. It was a game that overcame resistance to trying. I was having the time of my life — again.

Murphy's Law

"What can go wrong will go wrong."

Our flight school class was one of the last to be trained in three-point landings in World War II-era radial engine workhorses. My transition into jets followed fifty hours in the North American T-28 "Trojan," where I had earned a Standard Instrument Rating. The speed and altitude capabilities of the high-performance T-28 were an excellent introduction to the Lockheed TV-2 Shooting Star.

Most of the jet training instructors at NAS Memphis had seen service in Korea flying the first generation of Navy jet fighters — Grumman F9F-2 Panthers and McDonnell F2H Banshees, off straight-deck carriers. My instructor, Lt. Bob Jellison, flew Grumman F9F-6 Cougars off the USS Kearsarge (CV-33) in the Formosa straits in support of Nationalist Chinese evacuations from the Tachen Islands.

Four dual-pilot indoctrination flights in the TV-2 preceded solo time. Like my SNJ instructor Tom Weir, Lt. Jellison put me through the blindfold cockpit check. The TV-2 was much simpler than the SNJ or the T-28, with none of the complications of the piston-driven radial engine such as battery switches, magnetos, fuel-air mixture, cylinder head temperature, prop pitch, carburetor heat; it had fewer instruments and fewer levers. From the perspective of the pilot, the aircraft consisted of five functional systems: engine, flight controls, hydraulics, electrical, fuel.

Starting the engine was simplicity itself: an external auxiliary power unit employing an electric motor connects to the aircraft turbine with a shaft and gear which spins the main turbine shaft until sufficient air flows through the compressor and combustion chamber to light the engine. Fuel starts to flow, an igniter ignites it, and the turbine accelerates. After the SNJ and T-28's fire-belching radial engines the TV-2 hummed like an Oldsmobile's Hydra-Matic Drive. Flight controls were standard: rudders, elevator, ailerons. The hydraulic system provided aileron boost, lowered the landing gear and dive flaps, and ejected shell casings. Even with hydraulic failure the pilot could handle the aircraft manually and lower the landing gear by unlocking them and rocking the wings or pulling G's forcing them to drop. Electrical could be a problem, mainly because of internal fuel transfer boost pumps. The system that required constant pilot attention was fuel management. Lockheed's Skunk Works engineers had designed a beautiful, lightweight, streamlined aircraft, in which every major system except fuel could be accommodated *within* the airframe: hydraulic lines, electric wires, control cables were snaked through the fuselage and wings. But where was 825 gallons of jet fuel to be stored without compromising the aerodynamics? The answer: half of it in jettisonable wingtip fuel tanks and the rest in ten smaller fuel cells squeezed into the leading and inboard segments of the wing, all feeding into a 115-gallon fuselage tank located behind the cockpit, from which an internal boost pump injected the fuel directly into the engine supply manifold. All fuel that fed the turbine had to first be transferred to the fuselage tank for it to be usable.

The complexity of the TV-2's fuel system was in stark contrast to the simplicity of its design. The pilot would have to keep one eye on the sky and one on fuel management. Use of fuel had to be in sequence to maintain aircraft balance, beginning with tapping into the wing tanks, then the leading edge fuel cells, then the inboard wing group. If the pilot chose to manually control the sequence he could do so through a series of switches on the lower left console. He could choose *automatic* sequencing by putting all the fuel switches to the ON position, by which a series of float valves and boost pumps would automatically modulate fuel flow from the outboard tanks inward to the fuselage tank. For safety reasons, standard takeoff procedure was to use only the fuselage tank. The takeoff check list required the fuel transfer switches from the wing tanks, the leading edge group, and the inboard wing group to be in the down: "OFF" position. The logic was that in the event of a takeoff emergency all wing tanks would be isolated from the fuselage tank to minimize fire hazard. Students were drilled to turn on all the fuel switches immediately after becoming airborne and raising the gear. This was accomplished by moving a horizontal bar on the lower left console into the up position ("*gang-bar*"), placing all the fuel switches to ON.

The low fuel warning systems were a major design flaw in the aircraft. The fuel quantity gauge, intended to show the amount of fuel remaining, was set manually at the start of a flight and *subtracted* the fuel that flowed from the fuselage tank into the turbine. However, if the fuselage tank was not being replenished from the wing tanks, the fuel quantity gauge could read 9/10ths full, but the engine could be on the verge of flaming out. Two fuel warning lights on the instrument panel were also inadequate for the task. The first illuminated if the contents of the critically important fuselage tank dropped to less than 90% of capacity, signaling that it was not being replenished from the other tanks. The second came on if fuel flow from the fuselage tank to the engine fell to less than 3 psi. Under normal flight conditions the pilot would respond to these red lights by flipping on all the fuel tank supply switches. But if the pilot had been distracted and was not paying attention to the cockpit gauges and warning lights, a depleted fuselage tank would result in engine flame out. If engine flame out occurred at a sufficiently high altitude, the turbine could be restarted in a dive once the fuel flow was reactivated by turning on the fuel switches. But at low altitude, unless the aircraft was cruising at high speed, there would not be enough airflow to restart the turbine. The most critical period was after takeoff, when the aircraft was at low speed and low altitude.

Lt. Jellison drilled me on fuel management procedures, emphasizing how critical it was to gang-bar the fuel switches after takeoff. On the indoctrination flights prior to soloing the TV-2, the instructor was in a position to observe. On the solo flight, the student would be on his own.

Drake, Lace and I completed our indoctrination flights and had a free weekend before Monday's scheduled check rides and solo flights. Saturday night we drove into Memphis, where I introduced them to my fellow thespians at the Peabody. Three of the girls joined us at the bar, and took up Drake's invitation to meet us on the base Sunday for dinner at the Officers Club. Lace kept us in stitches, but we had to make it an early night because of our next day's flight schedule. We made a date to see them at the Peabody the following Saturday; which we didn't keep. On his solo the next day Drake failed to gang-bar his fuel switches after takeoff, didn't see the low fuel warning light, flamed out, and plowed into a stand of trees. I accompanied the casket as military escort for his funeral in Virginia.

Loss

When I returned from the funeral I found a note attached to my door in Bachelor Officers Quarters directing me to report to the base C.O. He encouraged me to go off flight status for a few days. Ordinarily, if a student pilot hits a snag the idea is to get him up in the air as soon as possible and work through the problem, but this was different. It was obvious to everyone that the accident had depressed me. This information got to the C.O. The flight surgeon signed a chit temporarily grounding me. At the base library I picked a thick book off the shelf: Thomas Mann's *Magic Mountain*, and flaked out on my bunk to read it. Chance could not have presented a worse choice. The hero, in his early 20's, while visiting a sick cousin in a mountaintop sanatorium is diagnosed with a serious illness and becomes a patient. The novel is an excursion into morbid philosophical introspection, portending the hero's death. I was rescued from this downward spiral by the Memphis Little Theatre Group.

Barbara Cason had decided to introduce her group of amateurs to the playwright considered to be the modern father of improvisation — Luigi Pirandello. She skirted the strictures on royalties by never advertising a performance, printing no tickets, and collecting no admissions. The company held "rehearsals" in the rooftop lounge of the Peabody Hotel, which was delighted with the arrangement since the patrons at the bar lingered to watch the actors perform. "The Twelve" got free rehearsal space and a built-in audience.

The play was "Six Characters in Search of an Author," a wacky scenario in which six strangers looking for an author barge into a theater company while it is rehearsing. The strangers are characters in an unfinished play and are seeking a playwright to finish their story. The resulting action is a total confusion of actors, the strangers and the director. What is reality and what is acting? What is pretense and what is fact? Taking part in these inventions proved to be a needed antidote. I soon returned to flight status, and by the end of the month wrapped up my jet indoctrination with five hours of night and actual instrument time.

My next assignment: Naval Air Station, Kingsville, Texas, for fifty hours advanced jet training in the Grumman F9F-2 Panther.

Kingsville

I reported to the Kingsville, Texas, Naval Air Station in late 1955 for the final phase of jet training. When I arrived, bad news was gripping the town; the railroad company had announced it was relocating its offices following a merger with Missouri Pacific Lines. Other than the Naval installation, for which residents were grateful, the local economy consisted of little but oil derricks, a gas pipeline, a cotton mill and a state college. Corpus Christi, forty miles northeast of Kingsville, offered some weekend diversion, but since Corpus was a military town new flight students like myself would not be able to compete with the regulars. The word around the base was get your time in and get out.

Up to this point I had logged 292 hours of flight time: 200 hours in the SNJ, 52 hours in the T-28, and 40 in the TV-2. Fifty hours in the single-seat Grumman F9F-2 "Panther" would complete my Naval Aviation training preceding assignment to a Fleet squadron.

Grumman Aircraft, like Lockheed and North American, had organized around the remnants of a predecessor company that was dismantled as a result of the Great Depression. Its founder, Leroy Grumman, inventor of the retractable landing gear, was another classic American aviation pioneer and industrialist. His World War II fighters and torpedo bombers were so sturdy sailors dubbed the company the "Grumman Iron Works." Even with that reputation, plummeting post-war military aircraft procurement required the company, like its competitors, to contract in size and adapt to the jet age.

The F9F-2 Panther, developed by the core group of young engineers assembled by Grumman, became the Navy's workhorse in Korea. I was eager to get into the cockpit.

Able, Baker

The F9F-2 handled as advertised — rugged, responsive, reliable; I understood why it was a pilot's favorite. Students were formed into sections and groups, briefed and led by instructors who had carrier experience in Korea flying the Panther. The weather was perfect, and I usually got in two flights per day. But with only a couple of flights left I received disappointing news. Instead of an assignment to a Fleet operating squadron I was ordered to report to the Chief, Naval Air Training Command in Pensacola for interim duty as a flight instructor — a "plowback." There was a surplus of Fleet pilots who had returned from the Korean theater, and the jet pipeline was jammed. I would have to await an opening. In the meantime, I would return to familiar territory for a stint in the rear seat training students.

In Pensacola I found myself in the SNJ again, training to be a flight instructor, sometimes flying with a pilot who remembered me from basic. Now, both wearing aviators' wings, we were members of the same fraternity. I roomed with three other instructors in a rented shack at the water's edge on Perdido Bay.

After qualifying as a flight instructor I was sent to Barin Field, where I was put into a rotation as a sort of utility player, filling in where needed. This suited me fine. It was so soon after my own basic training I felt I could handle any part of the flight syllabus. My first assignment was to give check rides to students who had received a "down." I held their aeronautical fate in my hands, literally.

Some student pilots on the verge of washing out had underlying ability, but could not demonstrate it in the cockpit. They knew the procedures, but were unable to execute. This had happened to my best buddy Rick Breitenfeld, who froze on landing approaches. When I told my instructor, Lt. Tom Weir, about Rick's landing block, he offered to take him up for a couple of flights. Instead of chipping at him impatiently, Weir calmly talked Rick through the process and built up his confidence. It worked. Rick passed his check ride, and soloed.

At one extreme were intimidating instructors with a low tolerance, at the other, those like Tom Weir, who gave encouragement. Both techniques had their merits, depending on the capabilities and temperament of the student. Some responded to task masters, who got the most out of them; others, like Rick, froze up. My natural inclination was to the latter camp. This produced positive results with many student pilots who had resigned themselves to being washed out. I found especially effective letting a student feel that what happened to the aircraft was up to *him*; that I wouldn't shadow him on the controls and wouldn't criticize each mistake. I kept my hands off the stick and talk to a minimum. One trick was to let the student take the aircraft to a point that was, for him, one of no return, such as stalling on landing flare out too high off the ground. Only until disaster was certain, as far as the student could imagine, would I take the controls. Adding full throttle and pushing the stick forward decisively would regain air speed in time to recover.

My tolerance reached its limits, however, with a check-ride student who gave up on a too-slow landing approach that could have resulted in a spin-out. I took over, recovered, and landed. When we got out of the aircraft I asked him what was going through his mind. He said, "I was praying." I confirmed the down and that was the end of him.

After a week of giving check rides I was assigned the first student for whom I would be primary instructor. Over the following ten weeks, fifty-three flying days in total, I logged 122 flights and 216 hours with forty-three students, eighteen as my primary students, and twenty-five for check rides. I had been pushing the schedule, some days logging five or six flights. This had earned me a reputation with the flight crew, as I often piloted the last plane to land, late in the day, the last plane for them to service.

After returning from a marathon double check ride with a marginal student I saw chalked next to my name on the flight status board a message to report to the base commander. What could this mean?

The base commander came right to the point, but not the talking to I expected: "Del Vecchio, we're going to be training students under a NATO agreement. I would like to assign you as their primary flight instructor. Is there any reason I shouldn't?"

"No, sir. I'd like to. Thank you."

The North Atlantic Treaty nations were in the process of standardizing military systems, which included sending student pilots through Navy flight training. Over the next several months, in addition to my regular flight students I was assigned student aviators from the Netherlands, France, Italy and Canada. The best were the Canadians, whose attitudes were closest to the Americans: they took control of the aircraft; they had more confidence, less caution; they were willing to take chances. The Italians were the least attentive, but the most fun. They enjoyed themselves.

For me, the most tangible impact of the NATO military compact was the conversion of the radio telephone alphabet. "Able, Baker, Charlie, Dog, Easy, Fox, George, How, Item, Jig, King, Love, Mike, Nan, Oboe, Peter, Queen, Roger, Sugar, Tare, Uncle, Victor, William, X-Ray, Yoke, Zebra," which had been imbedded in my brain in basic training, became "Alpha, Bravo, Charlie, Delta, Echo, Foxtrot, Golf, Hotel, India, Juliet, Kilo, Lima, Mike, November, Oscar, Papa, Quebec, Romeo, Sierra, Tango, Uniform, Victor, Whiskey, X-ray, Yankee, Zulu." I found myself having to translate from "Able, Baker," my native tongue, to "Alpha, Bravo."

The Rainmaker

Women foraging for husbands had lots of potential prey among the hundreds of green Ensigns arriving in Pensacola each year for flight training. Flight instructors were especially in demand. My roommates advised me to skip the social dances at the Officers Club or the Hotel San Carlos unless I was ready to have my wings clipped. Trader Jon's, downtown, was the usual starting place for their weekend bar circuit. That's where I met Joanne.

Joanne was sitting alone at the bar, seemingly disinterested in the crowd. I introduced myself. She responded: "You're from Boston." I had worked hard to conceal the accent, but she pegged it right away. She was studying method acting at the Dramatic Workshop in New York in a group that included Ben Gazzara and John Cassavetes, and had returned to Pensacola to take care of a sick parent. She was bored. I told her about my time with The Twelve, in Memphis, playing Joe in Saroyan's "The Time of Your Life," and the summer at the Boston College Summer School of Expressional Arts. Joanne could be intimidating. She was several inches taller than me, dressed provocatively, and had a sardonic wit. We hit it off.

An announcement in the *Pensacola News Journal* invited tryouts for the Pensacola Little Theatre's upcoming production of "The Rainmaker." Joanne read for the part of Lizzie Curry, a plain farm girl, and I read for the role of Bill Starbuck, the "Rainmaker." Starbuck is a con man claiming to be able to make rain; his fee — a hundred dollars. He enters into the lives of the drought-stricken farm community and the Curry family, where he brings out the beauty in Lizzie, delivering both rain and romance. Joanne and I were new faces and got the parts. The play was cornball but a crowd pleaser. Joanne and I became a team, continuing our on-stage romance off-stage, imitating ballroom dancers and clowning it up with my buddies, especially Frank Jarman.

FRANKLIN MAXIE JARMAN was the fun-loving scion of a prominent Nashville family. Its business was shoe-manufacturing. His passion was flying. Jarman was an operator. He arranged with the Mainside Aviation Maintenance Officer, a fellow Ole Boy, to check-ride an aircraft after overhaul before it was returned to flying rotation. He took me along for the ride on T-28 and TV-2 post-maintenance flights. Sometimes, when he was able to finagle an aircraft for me as well, we did formation acrobatics in TV-2s. Jarman could always be counted on to show up with a stunning girlfriend on a date. He kept his Beechcraft Bonanza at the

Pensacola civilian airport, which was a sure-fire way to impress the ladies. He had many.

Ensign Koga

I was summoned again to the base commander's office. What now? Did he know about my weekend check flights with Jarman?

"Lieutenant, I have been reviewing your record. You've been at this field for six months, is that correct?"

"Yes, sir."

"You've been training NATO students, correct?"

"Yes, sir."

"I assume you know about our military agreements with West Germany and Japan?"

"Yes, sir."

[This was false. I was paying no attention to geopolitics; I had been devoting myself primarily to having fun.]

"Good, because I have a job for you. We will be training the first Japanese naval officers to fly since World War II, and veteran German Naval Aviators who are to form a new German Naval Air arm. You will be primary flight instructor for the Japanese students and instruct the Germans on current instrument navigation. Any questions?"

"No, sir. Thank you, sir."

Only ten years later, our World War II adversaries had become our Cold War allies: the U.S. and Japan under a Mutual Defense Treaty signed in 1954, and West Germany in a 1955 expansion of NATO. I had been given an unexpected and interesting assignment.

ENSIGN KOGA WAS about five feet three inches tall. If he had applied to be a U.S. Naval Aviator he would have been rejected; he was three inches under the height minimum.

It took five backpads for his short legs to reach the SNJ's rudder pedals.

I became suspicious in my pre-flight briefings because he always replied "Yes" to my question as to whether he understood. I assumed he was being polite. He probably believed it would be an adverse reflection on my abilities as an instructor if he failed to understand, so I worked up a game with Koga. I tripped him up by giving contradictory instructions, all of which he "understood." Sometimes I would explain the procedure as specified in the flight manual; sometimes I would explain it incorrectly. Koga kept a detailed notebook written in tiny letters. He did his homework. He knew the procedures. When I was explaining something incorrectly, he furrowed his brow. After realizing the game I was playing, he flashed a huge smile. I got him to admit that he didn't understand when he didn't.

In the air, Koga was robotic. Provided there were no surprises, he was able to execute the rudiments of flight, but anything unexpected threw him. I had to repeat the initial, introductory flight, "T-1," three times, "T-2" twice. "T-4" would have been funny if it had not been so serious.

T-4 was to be a simple navigational flight — a rectangular pattern with four legs. The exercise was to observe how the wind affected the aircraft's track, and to correct for it so as to stay on course. After takeoff on Runway 15, south-southeasterly into the wind coming in over the Gulf, Koga climbed to 5,000 feet, trimmed up, and leveled off comfortably on course, on airspeed, and on altitude. The planned route took us over Perdido Bay, almost within sight of my beach pad. But instead of making a 90-degree turn onto the second leg, Koga remained on a south-southeasterly heading, crossing over the shoreline on a course that would have deposited us in Cuba if the SNJ had the fuel. As the sight of land receded behind us I quickly made a time/fuel/distance calculation, and decided to wait. I watched the back of Koga's gold-painted helmet motionless in the front cockpit, and said nothing. Finally, worried about the base commander's reaction if a wayward aircraft with no flight plan was reported, I decided to end wrong-way Koga's mission to Havana. I shook the stick, took the controls, made a 180-degree turn, and instructed him to return to home field, cutting short the flight. After landing, I acted routinely, said I was logging the flight as "incomplete," and that we would repeat it the following day.

Koga's father was Admiral Mineichi Koga, who succeeded Yamamoto as Commander in Chief of the Imperial Japanese Navy when Yamamoto's plane was shot down in 1943. A year later, Admiral Koga was killed in a crash. I was very concerned about young Koga's state of mind. A bad flight could discourage any young student; in Koga's case, the consequences of humiliation would be much worse.

The following day I asked Koga to brief *me* on how he was going to fly T-4. He produced a diagram of the route, which he had clipped onto his kneeboard, and explained the flight's every detail. The second time around he made the turns as planned, earning a "complete." I guessed that Koga had not realized the seriousness of his failure on the previous attempt at T-4, probably because he was accustomed to repeating flights. T-4 proved to be a turning point for Koga; he became more self-confident, even willing to ask questions. I felt good about my time with Koga; he was on his way to being an aviator.

Low and Slow

I spent weekdays in the back seat of the SNJ, a student pilot in the front, and occasional T-28 or TV-2 flights with Frank Jarman. Weekends, my roommates gave beach parties at our shack on Perdido Bay, featuring mint juleps mixed by Jim Burt, master of the "Split-S" evasive maneuver in our unauthorized dogfights; no one would pursue him on his hair raising dives and treetop-level pullouts. At bars, girls asked me if I could really make rain, after my buddies introduced me as "the Rainmaker." When it did rain, we played poker. The Pensacola Little Theatre group became a second home for me, like "The 3P's" in college.

Training young aviators was rewarding, especially those who developed confidence. Those that were most promising were stimulated by stress, whereas others, such as the student who responded to an emergency with prayer rather than action, washed out. After nine months of this routine I was assigned as an instrument flight instructor.

The Navy's instrument-trainer was the two-pilot, six passenger Beechcraft SNB, a 1930's vintage utility transport, two radial engines, twin rudders, classic three point, nose-high configuration, and 160mph/140knot cruising speed. In four weeks of instructor indoctrination I logged nearly ninety hours, a third of it night and instrument time, and had my first encounters with wing and carburetor icing.

I felt as if I was going backward in time. Instead of progressing from 600 mph/520 knots in the Shooting Star, punching through twenty-thousand feet of cloud cover in a few minutes to emerge into vivid blue sky above, I was chugging along in the clouds at a fraction of those speeds. Cruising at 40,000 feet, above the clouds, watching contrails, the jet pilot is free of constraints, while thousands of feet below, the conventional airman has to keep his eyes on his instruments, plot his track on a kneeboard chart, and constantly check his position against the clock. The compensation is teamwork between the pilot and co-pilot, a different experience from the solo jet jockey.

I developed new respect for "low and slow" aviators. I was now one of them. Then the Germans arrived.

Kriegsmarine

Outlined by the bright sky behind them, two figures entered the huge open doors at the far end of the Barin Field hangar and headed towards the briefing board in the center, where I awaited them. One was tall, and wore a long, black leather coat. The other was short and stout, and wore a jacket. The tall, imposing figure executed a quick, respectful salute as he introduced himself: "Commander Kluemper." His sidekick followed suit: "Lieutenant Commander Nagel." I was intimidated by their seniority and bearing. Commander Kluemper could have been Kurt Jurgens starring as the Luftwaffe ace in "The Devil's General," LCDR Nagel, a character out of "Casablanca." These were members of the World War II

"Kriegsmarine," flying Heinkels and Dorniers over the North Sea dropping parachute mines while I was a kid collecting old newspapers and tin cans for the War Effort. I maintained my composure and established our instructor/student relationship by immediately commencing the preflight briefing.

After the ground check I had Commander Kluemper take the left, pilot's seat, and I the right, co-pilot seat. LCDR Nagel sat behind us. I taxied and took off, with my customary explanation of every move. Even though I had accumulated four hundred hours in the SNB I was nervous about my aircraft handling as they sat quietly observing. Would *I* pass the test? At altitude I leveled out, trimmed for 140 knots, and turned the controls over to Commander Kluemper, whereupon I received a shock. He was having difficulty maintaining altitude, ranging a couple of hundred feet below or over, overshooting as he tried to correct, and in the process, failing to maintain airspeed. He was an ordinary mortal! LCDR Nagel was similarly rusty. On the debriefing they apologized, and I acknowledged that everyone requires time to get the feel of a new aircraft. They soon did, finishing the syllabus with a long night instrument flight to NAS Hutchinson, Kansas, which they managed confidently.

Although I took satisfaction in my duties, and had become proficient in night and bad weather instrument navigation, I was delighted when my long wait was rewarded:

I received orders to report to the Commanding Officer, Fighter Squadron Fourteen (VF-14), Naval Air Station Cecil Field, Jacksonville, Florida. Over a long stint in the Naval Air Training Command I had logged 1157 hours in the air on 569 flights, and been responsible for training 156 student pilots, half of whom as their primary instructor, and half for check rides. I was ready for the move.

Chapter 7

Fighter Squadron

Fighter Squadron Fourteen

I was put on the flight schedule the day after reporting to VF-14, spent the night studying the flight manual and the following morning in the cockpit of the F3H-2N "Demon" memorizing the instrument panel. Lt. Hamilton administered the blindfold cockpit check and took off beside me as wingman. We practiced section join-ups and touch and go landings. Over the next few days I flew formation with all the pilots in the squadron. The officers and enlisted personnel were sizing me up.

I was scheduled next for instrument refresher training in the Grumman F9F-8T "Cougar," the swept-wing successor to the F9F-2 Panther, lengthened to accommodate two pilots in tandem seating. I may have been new to this all-weather squadron, but not to instrument flying, having logged substantial instrument time in my 1500 hours over 800 flights as a student and instructor. I was quickly put into a regular flight rotation in the squadron's Demons.

The squadron was in the spotlight. It was preparing for deployment aboard the USS Franklin D. Roosevelt as the first carrier-based squadron equipped with an air-to-air radar-guided missile, the Raytheon Sparrow III. Raytheon engineers worked through the night with Gunnery and Avionics personnel as did engineers from McDonnell Aircraft in readying an aircraft's fire control system. It took thirty hours ground servicing of the Demon's radar and missile electronics for an average flight of about 1.5 hours airborne. The squadron was spit and polish to outward appearance, but on the inside operated more as a family. All hands understood the pressure we were under.

During the following three months we drilled relentlessly in the operation of the Sparrow III and the heat-seeking Sidewinder missiles, and spent hours of ground time simulating intercepts on blackboards and on our kneeboard slide rules. At this stage of the Navy's experience there was no established air to air intercept doctrine. We made it up on the fly, one aircraft playing bogey, the other flying the intercept. I enjoyed the challenge and became good at calculating the intercept solution: where to head and at what speed and altitude for the optimum release position; and flying the intercept with my eyes pressed into a hood which prevented sunlight from bleaching out the radar display. Although we younger pilots didn't have the older pilots' experience, we caught on quicker. Operations Officer Frank Murphy would schedule one of us to brief the visiting brass.

Fighter Squadron Fourteen was the Navy's longest actively-serving squadron. Its symbol was a top hat in a circle, and we made the most of it. Joanne negotiated a good deal with a Brooklyn hat manufacturer, who custom-made a batch of folding silk top hats for us. For the weekend of the top hat presentation ceremony she recruited some aspiring New York actresses. This occasion became a legend. The girls dangled their legs from the wing of a Demon as they posed for publicity shots surrounded by pilots in flight gear and top hats. At a pool party at the Officers Club, they topped off their bathing suits with top hats. The party continued at Ltjg. "Loc" Lynch's rented house in Jacksonville. The following morning, skipper O'Neill took one look at us and cancelled flight operations for the day. From then on, on cross-country flights, we stowed our folded top hats in a map compartment, and after landing, popped them open to exit our Demons with flair.

Rocks and Shoals

The officers of a fighter squadron relate to each other in two very distinctive ways. As pilots, they are equals, in all other situations the protocols of rank apply.

When the squadron Executive Officer, LCDR Roy Cornwell, called me into his office it was clearly official business. He said that when aboard ship on our coming deployment, commanding officers would exercise additional authority under the Uniform Code of Military Justice. It was very important, he said, that a squadron officer be trained as a Summary Court Martial so that this disciplinary responsibility could be administered from *within* the squadron rather than by an officer attached to the Air Group or the carrier. He said he had consulted with the skipper, and I was their choice to attend the Naval School of Justice at Newport, Rhode Island. He apologized that the course would take me away from squadron flying for several weeks but was confident I could handle the absence.

I was delighted. Newport was only seventy miles from Boston, meaning I would be able to visit my parents. I said "Certainly, sir. I would enjoy the opportunity."

My roommate in the Newport Naval Station Bachelor Officers Quarters was Lt. Tito Villarreal, Ecuadorian Navy. Our tiny room was spartanly furnished with a bunk bed and two small desks. Tito greeted me with enthusiasm. He told me he had been worried about who would be assigned as his roommate. When he learned it was going to be Ltjg. Del Vecchio, he felt better, and when I appeared, almost as short in stature as he was, he was much relieved. As far as he was concerned, I was a fellow Latin. Tito was lonely. When he turned in at night, he kept his light on, reading letters from home. I told him that my family lived in Boston, a couple of hours away by bus, and asked him if he would like to join me when I visited on the weekend, for a good Italian meal. He grinned from ear to ear.

Tito was being trained under an agreement between the Ecuadorian government and the United States, which maintained close military ties since World War II, when Ecuador declared war on Japan immediately after Pearl Harbor. Ecuador granted the U.S. base rights on the Galapagos Islands in the Pacific, six hundred miles west of Quito; the islands were strategically located for defense of the Panama Canal, a thousand miles to the northeast.

My parents were overjoyed at my visits while I was at the Naval Justice School, and embraced Tito as one of the family. My mother piled on the food and my father told all the jokes in his repertoire. He found a captive and willing audience in Tito.

FOR A HUNDRED and fifty years the officers and men of the United States Navy had been subject to the harsh strictures of the "Rules and Regulations for the Government of the Navy," enacted by Congress in 1800. Its origins were the prescriptions of the "Black Book of the Admiralty" — 14th century discipline administered aboard British warships, where flogging, branding, keelhauling, and putting men in chains were punishments applied in view of all hands, to deter anyone who might contemplate challenging the absolute authority of the captain.

The first rules of discipline enacted by the new American nation adopted British naval practice, declaring that offenses committed aboard ship "be punished according to the laws and customs in such cases at sea." Although the U.S. Congress prohibited flogging and other inhumane corporal punishments, the process and practice of publicly administered discipline remained the same. Naval justice was a harsh parallel of the English Common Law, based on applying like punishments for like offenses; a kind of common law of the sea. The "punishment of death, or such other punishment as a court martial may adjudge" could be "inflicted on any person in the naval service" who committed any one of twenty listed offenses, including not only desertion, cowardice in battle, or surrender, but also disobeying a lawful order of a superior officer, striking a superior officer, sleeping on watch, or leaving a duty station before being relieved. The severity of the regulations led to their being commonly referred to as "Rocks and Shoals" — break a rule and suffer severe consequences.

The centuries-old system of military justice broke down in World War II, when court-martials unduly burdened military commands. Over the course of the war two million military personnel were convicted by court martial. Following the war, a great debate took place in the Congress about modernizing military justice, pitting advocates of "discipline" against those of "justice." The result was the "Uniform Code of Military Justice," (the "UCMJ"), enacted in 1950, a compromise designed to preserve military discipline while administering it in a fair and efficient manner.

Under the UCMJ, Commanding officers retained the authority to appoint the jury (i.e., the members of the court martial), the judge (the "law officer"), and trial counsel. This power was balanced by pretrial investigation conducted by a neutral officer, the right of the accused to defense counsel, and appellate review by a civilian court.

At the lowest and most public level of discipline, commanding officers administered "non-judicial punishment" ("Captain's Mast"), where, for offenses not justifying convening a court martial, the sailor on report stood before the captain, in front of all hands, to hear his offense read and the C.O.'s decision. A commanding officer could also assign jurisdiction over charges against enlisted personnel to an officer designated as a "Summary Court Martial," or an accused could request his offense to be decided upon by a Summary Court Martial. Although this officer was authorized to prescribe stricter penalties than the commanding officer at Captain's Mast, a sailor on report sometimes chose this route, for a commanding officer making a decision in front of all hands might impose strict penalties so as not appear weak, whereas a subordinate officer serving as a Summary Court did not have this type of pressure and could exercise more latitude in balancing discipline and justice.

I finished the course, said goodbye to Tito, and returned to duty with my squadron. However, there was no time to put my legal training into practice, for I immediately joined my fellow VF-14 pilots in intensive live missile-firing exercises and field carrier landing practice preceding the squadron's deployment on the Roosevelt.

GITMO

VF-14 conducted rocket firing exercises over the Atlantic firing range east of Boca Chica Field at the Key West Naval Air Station, then deployed to Leeward Point Field on the Guantanamo Bay Naval Base for live-firing Sidewinder and Sparrow III "Battle Ready" qualifications. This earned pilots "E's" stenciled next to their names under the cockpit of a squadron Demon.

After qualifying, I was summoned again by the Executive Officer. This time it was informal. "Frank," he said, "the base C.O. has offered our squadron the use of his SNB if we want to shuttle sailors to Montego Bay, Jamaica, for liberty. This is a courtesy he provides for squadrons about to deploy aboard ship. However, he requires an experienced SNB pilot before he will entrust his aircraft to us. Will you do it?"

"Yes, sir. Of course, sir."

During our remaining time in GITMO I shuttled young sailors on liberty trips to Sangster Airport in Montego Bay. The round trip took from two and a half to three and a half hours depending on the winds. I left at daybreak — the last return late at night with a batch of youngsters flaked out asleep in the passenger cabin, oblivious to me at the controls. I consumed lots of coffee and No-Doz to stay awake on these solitary night flights piloting an old SNB as it droned on over a pitch black Caribbean Sea.

When the squadron returned to Cecil Field, LCDR Cornwell had another assignment for me. A petty officer on report for a drunken brawl at a local bar had requested a Summary Court Martial versus Captain's Mast, even though a Summary Court could impose greater punishment. This would be my first case as the squadron's Summary Court Martial Officer.

The petty officer had been up on Captain's Mast for the same type of offense several times before. I informed him of the process — that I would serve as prosecutor and defense counsel, and the penalties I was empowered to impose as judge: up to thirty days confinement, forfeiture of up to two-thirds of a month's pay, a reduction in grade, and sixty day's restriction. He was contrite, apologizing that when he gets drunk he doesn't realize what he is doing. His answer to my question as to what he thought would be a fair punishment was, "It's up to you, sir." I told him he was considered a good sailor, and I saw little deterrence value in a forfeiture of pay or a reduction in grade since his problem was drinking and losing control. I restricted him to base for sixty days, with no privileges at the Enlisted Men's Club or the Base Exchange. This is probably the punishment the C.O. would have imposed at Captain's Mast, but by requesting a Summary Court, the sailor avoided the humiliation of having to stand up again in front of the commanding officer and all the officers and men of the squadron.

Now designated "Battle Ready," we completed carrier qualifications on the Roosevelt and flew the squadron aircraft out to the carrier for operations in the Atlantic.

Carrier

The USS Franklin D. Roosevelt, (CVA-42), was a product of America's phenomenal military-industrial mobilization during World War II, but her commissioning in October, 1945 was a few months too late for her to see battle in the Pacific. Ten years later she was retrofitted with an angled deck, a British innovation which enabled an aircraft that failed to hook a wire on landing to add power and go around for another try. The two hundred fifty aircraft aboard the Roosevelt and the Intrepid, (CVA-11), delivered the punch for Carrier Division Two, U.S. Sixth Fleet.

The Roosevelt was the larger of the two carriers in the Carrier Division, with a complement of 4,104 officers and men, which swelled to more than 5,300, (twice the complement of a battleship), when the squadrons of the Carrier Air Group were aboard.

Carrier Air Group One — "Primus Princepes" ("First and Foremost"), organized in 1938 was the first of the Navy's tactical carrier-based attack groups. On the Roosevelt, the Air Group consisted of three attack squadrons, two fighter squadrons, and a photographic squadron detachment, one hundred forty aircraft in all, plus rescue helicopters.

Attack squadron VA-15 flew the Douglas AD-6 "Skyraider," a single-engine prop which could stay airborne for twelve hours, testing the endurance and the bladder of its pilot. VA-172, the "Blue Bolts," flew the small, maneuverable Douglas A4D-2 "Skyhawk." Heavy Attack Squadron VAH-11 flew the Douglas A3D "Skywarrior." Its symbol, the nucleus of an atom in a five-point star, indicated its armament.

The fighter squadrons were Marine All-Weather Fighter Squadron VMF(AW)-114 flying the Douglas F4D "Skyray" — logo, a skull superimposed on card suit symbols — (my buddy from Memphis, Fred Lacey, was in the squadron); and Fighter Squadron Fourteen (VF-14), the "Tophatters," formed in 1919, flying the McDonnell F3H-2N "Demon."

A detachment of supersonic Chance-Vought F8U-1P "Photo CRUSADERS," VFP-62 DET 37-59, and a detachment of rescue helicopters — HU-2, DET 37, rounded out the air group.

But before deployment, our squadron C.O. gave his pilots the weekend off to fly home.

Chapter 8

The Wrecking Ball

"O.K. boys," the Skipper said to the squadron pilots, "take your plane home for the weekend. See you Monday."

Home for me was Boston's West End, a thousand miles from our base at NAS Cecil Field, Jacksonville, Florida. I filed a direct flight plan for the South Weymouth Naval Air Station, south of Boston. This was a stretch for the fuel-hungry Demon, but I was counting on the jet stream to whisk me along.

I was down to only 800 pounds of fuel when the reassuring sight of the field's nineteen-story high blimp hangar came into view. I landed, parked the aircraft, climbed out of the cockpit, grabbed my overnight bag, filled out the post flight log, and changed into my dress blues.

A buddy picked me up at the base and we headed for the small house in South Medford, four miles from the West End, where my parents had moved when they realized what redevelopment would mean. Although I knew about the project I gave it little attention. I had left the West End far behind me, mentally as well as physically.

Our route took us on Embankment Road along the Charles River, under the el at Charles Street Circle, and past the Massachusetts General Hospital complex fronting Charles Street. Where the MGH complex ended, instead of the apartment buildings stretching from Allen Street to Leverett Circle, there was only devastation. The densely packed West End community had been reduced to rubble and the shells of buildings. Wrecking cranes lining the hill at the top of Chambers Street were finishing the job.

I told my buddy to pull over: *"This is my neighborhood!"* He stopped at the bottom of Chambers Street, which was impassable. I got out and began walking up Chambers through the rubble toward Saint Joseph's Church at the top of the hill.

The lower section of the West End, near the Charles River, had been leveled. The wrecking cranes were moving from north to south, along Allen, Poplar, Chambers, Leverett, Lowell and Staniford Streets, towards Cambridge Street at the foot of Beacon Hill. Although the buildings were gone, the streets signs bolted to light poles marked where they had been. As I walked up Chambers, I saw the signs marking what had been Portland Place, Auburn Street, Kinnard Ave., Brighton Street, Milton, Poplar, Poplar Place, Barton, Barton Ct., Spring, Ashland, Allen Court, McLean Ct., Hammond Ave., and McLean St. St. Joseph's Church, on Chambers Street between Allen and McLean, had been spared the wrecking ball. My building at 75 Chambers, opposite the church, had just been demolished, but number 73 Chambers was still standing. I recognized the pattern of the wallpaper high up on the exposed party wall as that of my bedroom. As I stood surveying the sad scene, with memories of my childhood on these streets overwhelming me, a pathetic old woman approached, stared at me, and asked "Frank Del Vecchio"? She obviously mistook me for my father. I said I was his son. She shook her head, mumbled something in Italian, and walked off.

The area beyond St. Joseph's, towards Cambridge Street, had not yet been demolished.

The buildings on Willard, Wall, Minot and Cotting Streets, Cotting Ct., Union Pl., Ransom St., Causeway St., Prospect Ct., Lyman St., Lynde St., Chambers Ct., Blossom Ct., Blossom St., Russell Pl., Parkman St., Eaton St., and N. Russell St. were still standing, most of them vacant, windows open, curtains blowing in the wind. Only a handful of people were in the streets.

I walked the short block to Eaton Street, where I grew up, to the corner of North Russell, opposite the Blackie Playground and Charlie Maccarone's store, my childhood hangout. I needed a memento. I grabbed a brick and pounded at the bolts that held the street sign to the lamppost at the corner of Eaton Street and North Russell Street, dislodging it. My buddy and I retrieved it, put it in the trunk of the car, and resumed our trip, now silent.

Power

My mother's kitchen was full of the smells of cooking: meat sauce, garlic, oregano, cheese, and the table was piled high with food. But my mind was on what I had just seen in the West End — devastation, rubble, abandonment.

My father said: "Yes, Frankie, everyone we know left long before demolition began. We knew the redevelopment was coming, and nothing could be done to stop it. As soon as the project was approved, the city stopped issuing building permits. When West Enders began leaving,

From "Walls Tumble in West End," *Boston Traveler*, August 14, 1958. The caption read, "Debris showers from the mouths of a steam shovel as demolition starts in earnest in the West End in the beginning phases of a giant redevelopment plan."

landlords rented cheap for a while, mostly to students and transients, but eventually gave up and demanded that their property be taken by eminent domain as soon as possible so they could get paid for it. The only ones left are some old timers who have nowhere to go; the rest are gypsies, squatters and winos."

My father told me his experience. His plan had been to buy a piece of property in the West End where he could live and work. He found the perfect building at the corner of Parkman Street and Blossom Street, owned by the shoemaker Thomas Nasti, who wanted to sell. My father intended to use the storefront as his workshop and live in the apartment upstairs. The selling price was $5,000, but the building needed repairs. We had a cousin who was a plumber, and relatives who could plaster, paint and wallpaper. My father estimated it would take an additional $5,000 for a roof and brickwork. He went to the Boston 5 Cents Savings Bank, and to the Shawmut Bank, where he had savings accounts, but no one would lend. A bank officer told him confidentially to look elsewhere for property; banks were not making loans in the West End because it was going to be taken for redevelopment.

My father had long been in favor of cleaning up the neighborhood and "building housing for poor people." I remembered an evening late in 1948, when my mother came back from a Mother's Club meeting at the Elizabeth Peabody Settlement House. She told my father and me that they had been shown plans for new housing to be built in the West End. I remember this vividly because of my father's reaction. He was disgusted with landlords who neglected their property, but because of their friends in City Hall, got away with it. The only way to get something done was to go hat in hand to a city councilor and ask for a favor. My father was not about to do that. He had great faith in the country, but no use for the local political gang.

Although he was ready to "Fight City Hall," the redevelopment project was something he couldn't contend with. He saw that the project was in the bag, gave up on Boston politics, and moved. He and my mother were among the thousands of West Enders who left years before

Also from "Walls Tumble in West End," *Boston Traveler,* August 14, 1958. The caption read, "...another huge shovel removes rubble after a building has been leveled at the corner of Milton and Leverert Streets."

demolition got underway in 1958. Now, his anger was under control; mine was building.

I sought advice from Dick Goodwin, who said to meet him for coffee at Howard Johnson's in Coolidge Corner. Dick, a summa cum laude Tufts graduate, spent a couple of years in the army, and at Harvard Law School repeated his summa cum laude performance. I told him about my experience that day, that my old neighborhood had been the furthest thing from my mind until I saw what was happening. It was too late to do anything, but I couldn't simply let this go. Dick said: "Frank, you don't have money or influence, but you have a brain. You should go to law school. That will give you power."

I accepted his advice, but told him I had an obligation for another year's service as a Regular Navy Officer, and would soon be leaving on a long Sixth Fleet deployment with my squadron. He said that shouldn't be a concern, and that he would introduce me to Dean Toepfer, Director of Admissions at Harvard Law School.

We hopped into Dick's VW Beetle and drove to Dean Toepfer's office, where he told Toepfer about our college friendship, and I told him my story. Dean Toepfer knew the Navy — he had served four years as an officer during World War II — and said that with my record he doubted I would have any problem being admitted to the law school. He advised me to take the Law School Aptitude Test and send in an application as soon as possible for admission to the class entering September, 1959; he would keep track of it.

Final Tour

On my return I told the skipper and the exec I had decided to resign my commission effective September, 1959 in order to enter law school. They understood my reasons and were supportive. I would be aboard the Roosevelt until then.

NATO exercises "Top Weight" and "Green Swing" revolved around the carriers Roosevelt and Intrepid. Fighter Squadron Fourteen's mission

Frank Del Vecchio, F3H-2N Demon, Fighter Squadron Fourteen, 1958.

was night and all weather defense of the Task Force against "attacking" French and Italian aircraft. The Italians flew Fiat G.91 single-seat fighter-bombers out of Practica di Mare Air Force Base outside of Rome. The intercepts proved incredibly uncomplicated because the Italians would fly directly towards our ships at a constant altitude and airspeed with no zigzags — (probably nursing their fuel supply). As "hot cat pilot" I would be launched on the first radar blip and vectored to make a head-on intercept with a Sparrow III. The Demons were configured with a radar memory that recorded the intercept, although, of course, the missiles were not armed. It took little effort other than keeping the target in the center of the scope, and releasing the missile ("Fox Away") as the circles closed. Because of the high rate of closure, only one bogey could be attacked at a time; the wingman had to be intercepted separately, with the option of "firing" another Sparrow, or employing a Sidewinder or cannon from behind. The Italians flew a very loose section — the leader and the wingman separated by a couple of hundred feet. After the dispatch of the section leader, I maneuvered to tail the wingman, simulated a kill with Sidewinder or cannon, then flew the Demon between the Fiats and added afterburner to pull away. Not until then were the Italians aware that they were goners.

The Dassault MD.454 Mystere was a more formidable target. If it had enough time to climb it could reach an altitude a couple of thousand feet higher than the Demon's service ceiling. The only way to bring down a high-flying Mystere was a head-on intercept, pitching up in afterburner to launch a Sparrow. These intercepts were successful because the Mystere was not maneuverable in the rarified air at those altitudes even if the pilot spotted the intercepting aircraft below. Invariably, the French pilots held constant altitude and airspeed with no clue they were being intercepted until advised by radio to return to base, their mission terminated.

One night I lost electrical systems on catapult launch, including cockpit displays, radio, and exterior lights. The bridge was unaware of my predicament since I was not being vectored on an intercept. I removed my oxygen mask and held a flashlight between my teeth in order to see the instrument panel. I had the airspeed indicator, needle ball and altimeter, but didn't have confidence in the other instruments. Fortunately, the cloudless night enabled me to circle overhead until the carrier turned into the wind to recover aircraft, whereupon I descended, fell into line behind the last aircraft in the landing pattern, and made a low pass by the island. This got attention. Immediately, I was flashed a green light from the bridge, and turned for a landing approach. I botched my first try, coming in too fast at too-low an angle of attack for the tailhook to catch a wire.

I did no better on the second pass — fearing that too slow an approach, nose high, risked a rapid sink rate that couldn't be arrested with power, which would result in my colliding with the fantail. But with my fuel gauge showing only 600 pounds, I decided to believe the angle of attack indicator and caught a wire on this third try. I checked in the aircraft, wrote up the problem, and had a routine debriefing by the Operations Officer; no one made an issue out of my two bolters.

One late afternoon, around dusk, the cloud tops brilliant white illuminated by the sun, while the sea below was already in the earth's penumbra, I wove my way down around the cumulus clouds on a visual approach to the carrier. I dropped the gear, lowered flaps, and released the tailhook for landing, when I saw the number "11" on the stack. I was

Piloting a VF-14 F3H-2N Demon, tail hook down, ready to catch a wire on the USS Roosevelt, CVA-42, 1958.

in the landing pattern for the Intrepid! I quickly added power, raised gear and flaps, wagged my wings and sped away, finally paying attention to my TACAN for a bearing on the Roosevelt. Like my excursion in the haze to Eglin Air Force Base when a flight student, this side trip escaped official notice.

The Roosevelt hit ports in the Mediterranean to give the crew liberty and show the flag:

Toulon, Genoa, Naples, Piraeus (Athens), Livorno, Palermo, Barcelona, Cannes. At Cannes, my buddy, helicopter pilot Mike Futterman, asked me if I would go up with him and take photos of coastal features. I didn't understand the purpose of the flight, but was happy for a helicopter ride in the right seat alongside Mike, and took my camera along. As soon as we began hovering over the coast, I saw what he had in mind — topless gals on the beach were standing and waving at us. Unfortunately, the pictures came out blurred; the vibrations generated by the Piasecki HUP-2 tandem rotors made the helicopter a noisy and unstable platform for a photo shoot.

In the same mail call that brought my Law School Aptitude Test results I received a letter from the Dean of Admissions that I had been accepted to the Harvard Law School entering class, registration September 3, 1959.

The Roosevelt turned over command to the USS Saratoga at Gibraltar, August 21, 1959, its Sixth Fleet mission ended, and took up a westerly course for the States. Even though it was peacetime, our air group had suffered the loss of two Marine and three Navy pilots, none from VF-14. Our squadron flew off the carrier Sunday, August 31, for Cecil Field, where a friend met me with the 1950 Ford I had left in his care. I turned in my flight gear, loaded the car, said my goodbyes, and headed for Cambridge.

Harvard Law

Professor Benjamin Kaplan opened his Civil Procedure class with a question in Latin, which was answered in Latin, instantly deflating the egos of the ten dozen first year law students arrayed in the hall. Then, he singled out a student in a back row, called him by name, asked him to rise and "state the case" assigned. There was nowhere to hide, for professors had before them a diagram giving the name of the student assigned each seat.

This was our initiation into the Socratic method. Before the student finished his synopsis, Kaplan interjected challenges, soon confounding him. When Kaplan asked if *anyone* could answer his questions, a couple of hands were raised, and the professor proceeded to engage these interlocutors in a dialogue. The depth and complexity of the exchanges was sobering to the rest of us. Although I had prepared for this first law school class I had not anticipated how quickly the limits of one's logic and composure could be tested and publicly laid bare. Kaplan's case discussions proceeded on an upward trajectory into a rarified intellectual realm few of us had previously experienced; college had not prepared us for this. They may have ranked first in class, but from the tension in their faces and their reluctance to raise their hands, it was clear my classmates were as terrified as I was.

In contrast to Kaplan, the trajectory of the questioning in Professor Clark Byse's Contracts classroom was inward and downward, burrowing into one's cerebral marrow. Byse relentlessly peeled apart a student's logic, unmasking incomplete preparation or fallacious reasoning, often reducing him to wordlessness, whereupon he would invite others to discuss where their hapless classmate went wrong. In the process, Byse, the monster, transformed himself into Byse the showman, using humor to relieve the tension.

Professor Charles Haar, in his course on Property Law, was no less formidable than Kaplan or engaging than Byse, but employed a different dialectic — one that was probably closer to the classical, guiding and stimulating the student's legal reasoning. I marveled at Kaplan's erudition and Byse's stagecraft but preferred Haar's style; his deadpan humor leavened the pressure. He was my favorite.

First year law subjects were grounded in English Common Law, a system for the resolution of disputes that had evolved since the twelfth century. The process helped unify the realm by holding the king's subjects accountable to a standard of behavior that applied to all, irrespective of station — a system of precedents to be followed in all cases of a similar nature.

Contract law evolved from judges' resolutions of disputes over agreements. No conflict was too trivial for the king's judges to adjudicate, even an argument over the ownership of a peppercorn. The law of Torts gave an aggrieved person an avenue to right a wrong without taking matters into his own hands. Property law established certainty in the control of the most valuable asset in the realm — land.

Reading cases, some of them dating back centuries, was more instructive than studying history texts, and infinitely more interesting. These were not theoretical or speculative excursions; the complainant who brought a writ for relief was party to a real controversy, an actual event. Even though the Colonies revolted, the industrial revolution changed the agrarian economy, and wars, famine, and pestilence intervened, the essential nature of disputes between persons remained the same.

It was evident from the course offerings that Harvard Law School in 1959 served as an integral component of the power structure: Estate Planning (geared to really *big* estates, i.e., the preservation and perpetuation of wealth); Tax Law (how to minimize tax liability); Property Law (how to control land); Trusts (ensuring the rich could dictate use of their money forever); Legal Accounting (recognizing the techniques of concealing accountability); Commercial Transactions (how to prevail in the competitive corporate marketplace); Agency (instruction in corporate safeguards); Criminal Law & Evidence (an examination of the impediments that can be interposed in uncovering the truth); Constitutional Law — the foundation for the entire edifice of American jurisprudence, essential to command the respect and retain the allegiance of the weak as well as the powerful.

In addition to the core curriculum, electives equipped the practitioner with the operational skills for maneuvering within the system: Antitrust, Real Estate Transactions, Corporations, Legal Remedies, Business Regulation, Labor Law, Commercial Law, Equitable Remedies, Administrative Law, Trial Practice.

This was exactly what I hoped for in my decision to give up my Navy commission. I was being introduced to all the levers of power. Whether one chose to steer the ship right or left, these were the propulsion mechanisms and the rudder controls necessary to make way. In the crucible of the law school environment, my fellow students were neither minions of the powerful nor defenders of the weak, irrespective of the inevitable outcome of their training: that he who pays the piper calls the tune. Notwithstanding the certainty that the overwhelming majority of graduates would be employed by the legal establishment — firms that dominate the practice of law, sustained by monied interests — for the time being my classmates could be the most intense critics of appellate court decisions they believed went wrong. In Criminal Law, Moot Courts, and in Constitutional Law discussions, they could be compelling advocates for justice.

I roomed with Chicagoan Nick Karzen, and Neil J. Cohen, from Shaker Heights, Ohio, in a low- rent flat a few blocks from the law school, at the corner of Concord and Huron Avenues across from a gas station. They presented me with a bicycle after I sold my old Ford to save the cost of auto insurance. For income, I helped out my father at his Tufts and Dartmouth football concessions. As in college, classmates welcomed the invitation to enjoy a good Italian meal at my parents' house in Medford.

I WAS READY for a summer break. I joined my friend Gordon Lapides on a long drive to Berkeley, where we audited courses. That summer of 1960 the Berkeley campus was stirred up by a militant movement, "SLATE," organizing for civil rights. Gordon and I dove in and accompanied the group to Los Angeles for a demonstration at the Democratic National Convention. Sunday, July 10, the day before the convention opened, Martin Luther King, Jr. addressed a large crowd, most of them students, outside of the L.A. Memorial Sports Arena convention site. Gordon and I paraded around the perimeter carrying "FREEDOM NOW" signs, calling on passersby to join us.

That evening, at a NAACP rally in the Shrine Auditorium, the candidates for the party nomination addressed a capacity crowd. Senator John F. Kennedy, who had represented my West End district in Congress, was tentative about a civil rights plank and drew boos from the crowd. Hubert Humphrey and Adlai Stevenson did better. Lyndon Johnson and Stuart Symington didn't appear to be contenders. The next day, hearing Boston accents, I mingled with a group of party delegates from Massachusetts, who managed to get me and my friends into the convention hall with them. When Stevenson's name was put into nomination we waved "ADLAI" posters in the loudest demonstration of support for any candidate. The moment of euphoria was brief; Kennedy won the nomination on the first ballot. We left for Berkeley before his acceptance speech the next day at the L.A. Coliseum.

THE PRESSURES OF the second year at the law school did not compare with the first, unless you happened to be in the wrong classroom. One of the electives I chose was Professor Archibald Cox's course in Agency Law. Kaplan, Byse, Haar, might have been demanding task masters, but Archibald Cox was cruel. If a student's logic proved superficial or he was unprepared, Cox kept him standing and twisting in the wind. Kaplan had been a member of the prosecution team at the Nuremberg Trials. We joked that if Cox had been on the team more of the defendants would have taken Göring's route — suicide.

In addition to second year law school electives I audited courses in the University: Professor Carl Friedrich's lectures on political propaganda and public opinion; Prof. Thomas Schelling's seminar on war gaming and conflict behavior; a seminar on local government given by professors Edward Banfield and James Q. Wilson; and the Defense Policy Seminar conducted by professors Henry Kissinger, Thomas Schelling and William Barton Leach.

Friedrich's concern was how easily propaganda could be used to shape opinion. Schelling's thesis was that mutual disclosure could serve as the avenue to negotiate Great Power nuclear weapons agreements. I couldn't decipher his equations, but his examples were straightforward: Nuclear miscalculation could be avoided if the U.S. and the Soviet Union traded military information starting with small, verifiable increments, adding more to a point that would enable them to avoid panic if an aberration occurred.

At one end of the spectrum were Banfield and Wilson, who challenged us to refute the case they made for the political boss system: that old-line ward bosses produced better results than good-government scientific management because if they didn't deliver on their promises they would be tossed out of office. They required results if an appointee was to keep his job; a contractor had to *perform* in order to be awarded more work.

At a higher altitude was the Defense Policy Seminar chaired by Kissinger, who invited international leaders such as Pierre Mendes-France, (former French Foreign Minister and later Prime Minister), high-ranking military officers such as retired General Maxwell Taylor, (Army Chief of Staff in Korea and later Chairman, Joint Chiefs of Staff), and provocative analysts such as Herman Kahn ("On Thermonuclear War," arguing that for nuclear deterrence to be credible, the U.S. had to have a "second strike" capability — the genesis of the Cold War nuclear doctrine of "Mutually Assured Destruction," MAD). Kissinger, the historian, demonstrated how to disarm a guest by putting himself in the other's shoes and establishing rapport. His technique was the reverse of the adversarial process. Schelling, the economist, pursued rationality — a dialogue exploring unintended consequences. Leach, the law professor, a retired Air Force General, employed challenge and confrontation.

I SPENT THE summer between my second and third year at law school going door to door in Boston's low-income Roxbury neighborhood interviewing residents in a survey funded by a Federal urban renewal planning grant. [Family surveys were required for approval of a project involving relocation; Roxbury was a target for redevelopment.] These summer jobs were parceled out through a political patronage system that gave city councilors and State reps a way to reward their supporters. As window-dressing, the city's redevelopment agency had hired several college students, including two Egyptians enrolled at Harvard's Architecture and Planning School, and me. The three of us formed an interview team which soon drew the anger of the supervisors because we completed more than our quota of surveys a day. Most of the teams produced one, or at best a couple of interviews a day, fabricating most attempts at entry as "failed." They played the Boston political game: Show up for attendance, go out into the field, and after racing through one survey disappear, returning at the end of the day to sign out. To the dismay of the higher-ups our team averaged three surveys a day.

Hosni Iskander, and Salah El-Shaks, dark-skinned Egyptians, took the assignment seriously, as did I. Residents of the black neighborhood opened their doors to us, invited us in and sat around answering our questions. The conversations went far beyond what was required on the forms. By the end of the summer we had turned in a couple of hundred survey forms and learned a great deal about the community.

On our last day our supervisor, Joe Charyna, took me aside, handed me a fat manila envelope, and told me to keep quiet about it. Charyna, an activist in Boston's growing Ukrainian community, had supported city clerk John B. Hynes in his 1949 campaign for mayor against James Michael Curley. After Hynes's upset victory, Charyna was rewarded with a city job. In 1957, on the eve of West End demolition, Joe had been put in charge of family relocation, working out of the old city Health Unit on Blossom Street.

Now, in the summer of 1961, the West End in rubble and everyone gone, he entrusted his collection of project clippings to me.

CHAPTER 9

CITY HALL

Every spring, recruiters from major law firms converge on Harvard Law School to interview graduating third-year students. I signed up and went through the process, but my heart wasn't in it. When a couple of firms wanted to schedule me for follow-up interviews I began to worry. I sought advice from Professor Haar, in whose Land Use Planning Seminar I had written a research paper on urban renewal. I had cross-registered in the Harvard Architecture and Planning School for seminars with Martin Meyerson and William Alonso in city and regional planning, and needed only a few more credits to get a masters in city planning degree. I asked Professor Haar if he would sign a letter of recommendation for me for the Graduate City Planning program. He dismissed this immediately, saying "Frank, you have all the education you need. Now is the time to put it to work." He telephoned Justin Herman, the redevelopment director in San Francisco, and Ed Bacon, Philadelphia's planning director, but they were out of the office. He reached Ed Logue, Boston's development director, gave me a nod while on the phone, and told me I would be scheduled for an interview with John Bok, Logue's legal advisor.

John Bok was a member of an old-line Boston law firm and had taken a leave of absence to serve as legal counsel to Edward J. Logue, the highly visible new chief of redevelopment for Boston. Bok, along with planners and architects from around the country, had been attracted to Logue's promise of a new brand of urban renewal: "Planning with People."

I had reservations, for this was the same agency that had obliterated the West End. Bok reassured me. He lived at the top of Beacon Hill on

Pinckney Street, where he watched as my old neighborhood, only blocks away, was under the wrecking ball. He explained that Mayor Collins had split the redevelopment agency into two independent operating units. The old guard, which had engineered the West End project as the urban renewal division of the Boston Housing Authority, was now responsible only for previously approved projects. They operated out of a different building, with their own staff, director, and general counsel. New projects, and the city's planning and zoning functions, were under Development Administrator Logue's command.

Bok knocked on the door connecting his office to Logue's, who greeted me with Irish charm and Yale Law School polish: "Del Vecchio — Navy carrier pilot, and a student of Charlie Haar's. I guarantee you this. There will be no repeat of the West End under me. If I ever go wrong, call me on it. I was a bombardier; you can shoot me down if I fail you." He was impressive. I felt he would hold his own in the cutthroat politics and power struggles in Boston. Moreover, because of the public backlash against the West End's demolition, he could not afford to renege on this pledge if he was to succeed. We shook hands; I would work as staff attorney under John Bok. Next step — clearance by John McMorrow.

McMorrow was Mayor John F. Collins's man at the Boston Redevelopment Authority. After McMorrow's defeat in the 1959 mayoral primary he had thrown his support to Collins, the underdog. All applicants for BRA jobs had to get his O.K. The Boston patronage system had not disappeared merely because Collins was a reform mayor and Logue projected a professional mystique. McMorrow was an essential intermediary.

He came right to the point: "Frank, I checked you out — Boston Latin, English High, Tufts. My job is to protect the mayor, which I do by getting qualified people. We take care of our friends, but they have to send us people who can get the job done. There are grumblings in city hall that we're bringing in too many outsiders. You'll help — you're a Bostonian and you have credentials.

"I'm going to be blunt. I'd be surprised if you don't hold a grudge over the West End project. Here, you'll be in contact with the people responsible: Kane Simonian — the front man for the project as urban renewal director for the Boston Housing Authority, John Conley, BHA general counsel, and the developer Jerry Rappaport. You know how he orchestrated the project as confidential secretary to the previous mayor. He's in the office from time to time."

I told McMorrow that I appreciated his frankness but he needn't be concerned. Although the destruction of the West End was burned into my memory, I'd support Logue and the mayor.

John F. Collins had won an upset victory over state senate president John E. Powers in a contentious 1959 Boston mayoralty election. Collins's inauguration pledge to cut spending and cut taxes was immediately dashed when his nemesis Powers, presiding over the state senate, summarily dismissed Collins's property tax relief bill.

Collins had to find some other way to deliver on his promise of "Operation Revival." Resurrecting the urban redevelopment program of his predecessor, though risky, could be the answer.

He turned for help to fellow mayor Dick Lee of New Haven, who loaned Collins his development administrator Ed Logue to size up the possibilities in Boston. Logue had earned a reputation as a "public money man" for his success in mining federal dollars. As New Haven's urban renewal czar, Logue excavated a mother lode of federal funding, obtaining more redevelopment grant funds per capita than any city in the country.

Logue had mastered the complexities of a federal funding formula that enabled a city to finance municipal development with federally-insured loans whose interest costs, along with the cost of city improvements, would be two-thirds paid for by urban renewal grant funds. An artfully contrived urban renewal program could use federal renewal loans and grants to finance public works, fire and police stations, schools, parks, municipal parking garages and other city facilities.

But federal urban redevelopment money didn't rescue New Haven's collapsing downtown economy. Logue's five-year blitzkrieg produced only a huge municipal parking garage in a barren wasteland that had been home to immigrants and blacks before demolition. He needed a new and larger canvas on which to display his talents. Boston gave him a second chance.

Politics First, Planning Second

Logue arrived in Boston March, 1960 to assess the possibilities. Political calculations were the first priority. That meant the Mayor, the Church, and The Vault.

Collins's campaign backers: the banks and property owners dubbed "The Vault," (they met in a bank), quickly signed on for redevelopment projects downtown, the waterfront, and the Prudential Tower site in the Back Bay, plus razing old Scollay Square and the remnants of the West End on its periphery for a sweeping Government Center showcase featuring a new City Hall and public plaza. With this green light, Logue put into action a plan to consolidate all legal authority over planning and zoning power in his office.

More challenging was rounding out the Boston program with neighborhood renewal projects — a political marketing and Federal funding necessity. Even though a broad canvas for redevelopment had been provided in 1950 when the planning board designated 2700 acres of the city "slum, blighted, or decadent," without Church approval, ethnic Catholic neighborhoods were untouchable. This ruled out Irish South Boston and the Italian North End and East Boston. Charlestown, the South End and Roxbury were the most promising targets of opportunity. In the wake of West End clearance, however, a debacle that had alienated the city's neighborhoods and, if repeated, would be fodder for city councilmen grandstanding, the Mayor and the Cardinal hedged. It would be up to Logue to be out front. The Mayor's people were placed on every project team, the editor of the diocesan newspaper, "The Pilot," was appointed chairman of the Redevelopment Authority, and every aspect of urban renewal planning for Catholic Charlestown would have to be approved by its three Monsignors.

Charlestown was a proud Irish enclave losing population, where renewal could be sold as its savior. The South End, a mixed social and racial neighborhood close to downtown with a valuable historic housing stock in disrepair, had no ethnic political clout and could be promoted as a textbook exercise in planning and preservation. Roxbury, transitioning rapidly to a wholly Black population, was an area ripe for government action provided it was not perceived as Black removal. This required nurturing a nexus of local Black leadership. Logue's bag of tricks featured federal urban renewal funds to replace old schools, fire stations, aged water and sewer lines, streets and facilities in these dilapidated sections of Boston, with nothing initially out of pocket for a city on the edge of bankruptcy. Maximizing federal project grants required that project boundaries be drawn as broadly as possible, but most important was organizing neighborhood support and quelching opposition; in short, a planning process on the political campaign model.

Thanks to the former mayor's operatives, a promising nucleus of grass roots support in each of these communities had already been identified: in Charlestown, members of a self-help group anxious to stop the exodus of the younger generation from the "Town"; in Roxbury, an emerging Black leadership which saw its opportunity to become politically relevant; in the polyglot South End with its skid row, bars, rooming houses and homeless, earnest social reformers. Logue walked the neighborhoods, cultivated local leaders, impressed them with his insights and commitment to their goals, allaying fears with his urban renewal sales pitch: *"Planning with People."* The stage was set. But the curtain was poised to fall even before the play opened.

The Road Gang

A shock went through City Hall when Federal highway engineers unveiled plans for a northward extension of Interstate Highway 93 cutting directly through Charlestown. This would kill the Charlestown project and doom a scenario that depended on renewal of three ethnically diverse neighborhoods: White Charlestown, Black Roxbury and the multi-racial South End. Charlestown was the political linchpin in the strategy. The highway route had to be changed. Logue got the rescue assignment.

The engineers had drawn a straight line for an elevated segment of the interstate highway from the Central Artery at North Station, over the Charles River, running the entire length of Charlestown to Sullivan Square and severing a quarter of the town in the process. This alignment would destine Charlestown to become another victim of the interstate highway program — a tangle of highway interchanges, access ramps, and truck marshaling yards presided over by the Bunker Hill monument's granite obelisk.

Collins was up against it. Cities had no legal authority over the Interstate Highway System's use of eminent domain powers. Unless Congress intervened, Federal bureaucrats could do as they chose. But even if the mayor were to ask Boston's congressional delegation for help it would have little influence, as the argument that the highway would "blight" Charlestown was off the table. Soon after Congress's enactment of federal slum clearance legislation in 1949, former Mayor Hynes, setting the table for redevelopment projects benefiting favored developers, got the city planning board to declare much of the city, including Charlestown, "blighted" and "decadent." The city would be hard pressed to argue the contrary. Moreover, that declaration was legally necessary to justify a Federally-assisted renewal project. Logue had to find another way.

Logue's strategy was to get consensus on a master transportation plan that would push the highway alignment west, above Boston & Maine Railroad rights-of-way, sparing residential Charlestown. This would require negotiating with the agencies controlling road, rail and transit routes through the City of Boston — the local "Road Gang." If the plan had something in it for everyone, it stood a chance.

Logue conceived of a vehicle to implement his strategy — the "North Terminal Area Policy Committee," which would be chaired by the one entity that was not a competitor for transportation projects — the City of Boston. Latching on to the Federal highway project provided the agencies many opportunities for capital projects. Each agency signed on because it could not risk being left out of the action. Mayor Collins was appointed chair. Logue then maneuvered the committee to agree on a master concept plan showing a realigned I-93 through the Boston & Maine rail yards and a relocated rapid transit line running alongside it. With this concept approval in hand, Logue could turn his attention to getting his agency up and running and leave the details to staff and attorneys.

Fresh out of law school in June, 1962, my first assignment at the Boston Redevelopment Authority was to formalize the legal obligations of this plan. How was a young green attorney to get these seasoned potentates to agree? The task proved to be not as difficult as I feared: I had an advantage — a plan, a blueprint to follow, while each agency had only its part of the plan to worry about. The engineers I dealt with approached negotiations as a problem to be solved, not something to fight. The real test would be with their bosses, the agency heads, over the issue of giving up power.

The Massachusetts Port Authority was the most daunting hurdle. Although established fifteen years prior, it was still in the process of expanding its sway. In contrast with the City of Boston, saddled with constraints over what it could do, including the Governor-appointed Boston Finance Commission, (originally set up to keep an eye on Boston Irish pols), the MPA operated as a special purpose agency with independent bonding authority that gave it great power in the construction, financial and political arena.

The MPA controlled Boston's Port, the airport, and connecting tunnels and bridge. It had eminent domain authority and could call the shots. The best the mayor could do was nip at its heels, such as throwing up roadblocks to the use of city streets by contractors' trucks, and denying street closures for access ramps. The transportation plan required reconfiguring access ramps to the MPA's toll bridge over the Mystic River between Charlestown and Chelsea. The ramps had to thread through the narrow and historic Charlestown Streets, in an Irish community boasting three Monsignors and ready to show its anger if trampled on.

This gave Logue a toehold in negotiations. He let the MPA know that if it decided to act unilaterally it would have a fight on its hands. But he also offered an olive branch. He was willing to take the heat on land takings for approaches to the new access ramps to the Mystic River Bridge using the city's eminent domain authority as part of the Charlestown Urban Renewal Project. The MPA bought the deal. Next up: the Boston & Maine Railroad.

As Logue anticipated, as far as the B&M was concerned it all boiled down to dollars and cents. Railroads were in a downturn due to trucking industry inroads on their freight business. We knew the B&M needed money because it had pleaded with the mayor for tax relief. Logue's route would give them a windfall of U.S. Bureau of Public Roads purchase of RR rights of way. As important as the highway alignment was, however, Logue also needed the B&M to agree to use of its rights-of-way as the location for a relocated Charlestown El as part of a Federally-funded urban renewal project. This all depended on how persuasive he could be with the Federal Urban Renewal Administration.

The Charlestown "El"

The 60-year old Charlestown "El" elevated rapid transit structure was a behemoth that snaked along Main Street for the entire length of the Charlestown peninsula, the same route taken by Paul Revere in the early morning hours of April 19, 1775 to warn colonists that British regulars were on the way to Lexington and Concord. A marvel in its day, the El stood only feet from the tenements alongside. The steel wheels of the trains screeched on the curves; its supporting columns proved immovable hazards for drivers below. Townies bragged about their ability to evade police pursuit by speeding beneath these legs of steel.

The El had exacted its toll. Apartments alongside were either vacant or in disrepair; landlords would not make improvements to these low rent properties. The conditions along Main Street discouraged any investment in the town. If there ever was a "blighting influence" the El was it! Neighborhood leaders told Logue there could be no hope for the community unless the El was removed, and they would not support an urban renewal project unless it included the relocation of the El.

With the MPA and the B&M relying on his promises to obtain Federal funding for the city's part of the deal, and the Charlestown project hanging on El relocation, Logue now had to deliver. He turned to his friends at the Federal Urban Renewal Administration. Not only would the City of Boston's renewal program require huge funding earmarks and planning advances for Logue's wide-ranging vision, the earmarks would have to include an unprecedented $12 million for the relocation of the Charlestown El. If the Feds didn't come through, Charlestown would be carved up by roadways and Boston could kiss goodbye to community renewal.

Logue made the case that urban renewal was in jeopardy nationwide and needed a new model on a scale the American public would notice. Boston would be that model.

The country had soured on a program that was bulldozing poor and minority neighborhoods. Congressmen who had voted for the Housing Act of 1949 were now in a mood to terminate urban renewal (and along with it the agency and its personnel). Logue offered a new image — urban renewal that would *preserve*, not destroy neighborhoods, developed through a process of *"Planning with People."* He described how the national press would be attracted to projects in Charlestown, Roxbury, and the South End — three racially distinctive Boston neighborhoods. Charlestown, a political necessity for the package, could not be renewed without funding for El relocation, and its failure would end the vision of urban renewal for poor neighborhoods, White and Black.

Logue won the day. Federal administrators bought his argument and agreed to a preliminary $30 million funding earmark, but explained he would have to mobilize much broader political support for final approval to use Federal urban renewal funds for "El" relocation.

With the principal actors now signed up, the remaining state agencies fell into line, followed by the U.S. Bureau of Public Roads. Boston had become a player in the road gang's monopoly game.

Skyhawk

In the summer of 1962 I joined newly formed Naval Reserve Jet Attack Squadron VA(J)-911, flying the Douglas A4B Skyhawk out of the South Weymouth Naval Air Station.

On weekends, I was back at the controls of a carrier jet, buzzing the beaches along the New England coast. When we weren't dive-bombing picnickers who ignored the "DANGER, LIVE BOMBING" signs on the Navy bombing range at "No Man's Land" island off Martha's Vineyard, we were practicing high speed tree-top-level attack runs.

The Skyhawk was a compact Aston Martin compared to the Demon's muscular Corvette.

Although it was only half the size of most attack aircraft, its two 20mm cannon, bomb and missile stores provided equivalent punch. Its secret capability was a tactical nuclear weapon.

The nuclear attack mission gave pilots an excuse to perform daredevil maneuvers on training flights. A typical practice mission was to simulate a launch from a carrier off the coast, climb to altitude, then dive to wave top level for the run to the target. Over land, navigation was visual. Holding a constant airspeed, track to target was accomplished by spotting landmarks at preplotted three-minute intervals. Upon reaching the "initial point," the pilot arms the device and focuses on an illuminated fire control sequence cockpit display, then pulls the nose sharply up in a constant G, controlled climb, and releases the "Shape" on a parabolic arc. After release he executes a three-quarter loop ending in a modified Immelman 180-degree course reversal near the deck, and races away at tree-top level. Most of the training routes were along the Maine coast, penetrating it at low altitude for simulated targets in wilderness areas. In summer months unsuspecting beachgoers were unaware until we roared over them.

I drove a Triumph Motors TR-4 roadster with a removable hard top, a roll bar, and full four-point shoulder harnesses and seat belts courtesy of the riggers at South Weymouth. Frequently, when he was late for a meeting, Logue would ask me for a ride. I could usually oblige since I was able to squeeze the TR-4 into a tight parking space near our City Hall Annex office. I would instruct Logue to strap in, and then drive off at breakneck speed through Boston traffic. Logue's body would tense but he would never murmur an objection.

During negotiations for railroad rights of way, I took photos of the Charlestown rail yards and highway approaches to the Mystic River Bridge, from 10,000 feet. I was flying visual flight rules, and all it took was clearance from Boston Air Traffic Control to circle my Skyhawk over the city. Ten thousand feet was above Logan Airport traffic approaches and below the jet routes. I had the skies over Boston to myself. Logue, who had flown as a bombardier, one-upped the attorneys for the B & M in these negotiations by springing on them my 35mm slides of empty railroad yards.

Eliminating Rivals

I met Marian Seidner at a Cambridge party late in the summer of 1962 and knew immediately she was the one — smart, dark humor, an aura of mystery, and I made her laugh. I confided in her friend, Barbara Raye, that I wanted to marry Marian, but she was inscrutable and surrounded by other men. I was serious. She wasn't. I asked Barbara what she thought. She said, "Go for it!"

I set out to eliminate my rivals.

Tim Hobbes was a handsome eighteen-year old Texas cowboy whose family owned a thousand square miles of West Texas. Tim was hanging around Harvard and latched onto Marian. He was sweet, innocent, lovable and good company. He amused her. My plan was to lay my cards on the table. I met Tim for coffee at the Midget Restaurant, across the street from Marian's 1713 Massachusetts Avenue apartment. I told him straight out that I wanted to marry Marian; that I was twenty-nine, had been a Navy pilot for five years, had my law degree, and was intent on making Marian my wife. I contrasted this with his situation: He was nine years' younger than Marian and still finding out about himself and life. Tim sat mute, his face a blank.

Tim stopped dropping by Marian's apartment as he used to. Marian wondered what had happened to him. I said nothing.

Dan Hughes would be a challenge. He was a surgeon at Peter Bent Brigham Hospital, dry wit, mature. They shared a bond. He was a constant presence. I decided to outlast him. The three of us sat around Marian's apartment, drank bourbon, listened to records, and talked. And talked. I was dug in. Dan's appearances became less frequent. Marian emptied a bureau drawer for me, and I moved in. Mission accomplished.

I dreamt up things to impress her. I drew a map plotting all the bars I knew within a ten mile radius of Boston. We started downtown, in territory that was familiar to me from my summer as a runaway, and moved outward in concentric circles ending up at the Paradise in Revere — the pits, and the end of the opening scenario. I did my Gene Kelly dance routines and my Ho Chi Minh imitations. I took her home to meet my parents. I was surprised when they were not as demonstrative as usual.

On the way back to her apartment, Marian said it was obvious; they disapproved of her because we were living in sin. I said that could easily be remedied — she could marry me. She tensed: "Not possible." She didn't explain. Yet she looked forward to my arrival after work, and we were constantly together. I tried again. She replied, "Frank, I'm not ready for marriage; not yet at least." I was undeterred.

Anschluss

In April, 1938, Hans and Alice Seidner, with their children Marian, Susan, their nanny, Tetta, and older brother, Frank, left their home in Jihlava, Czechoslovakia for vacation in Laurana, Italy, on the northern Adriatic. Three year olds Marian and Susan were identical twins, Frank was three years older. They took no more luggage than a typical European family on holiday. Hans, however, had no intention of returning.

Hitler's annexation of Austria in the March 12, 1938 Anschluss, confirmed Hans Seidner's assessment that Czechoslovakia would be next. Already, travel restrictions were in place, and Jews, especially, were under scrutiny. Hans, and Alice's father Hugo Hanak, devised a plan of escape.

The Seidners and the Hanaks were prosperous industrialists, with textile mills in Brno, the capital of the Moravian region of Czechoslovakia, which had become part of the Austro-Hungarian Empire in the mid nineteenth century. Though historically Jewish, the families were culturally Austrian. They spoke German, attended opera and frequented galleries in Vienna, seventy-five miles south.

Hugo Hanak and his wife, Stephanie, left first, for a villa in Laurana. He had moved art out of the country and put money in Swiss banks. Hans, Alice, nanny Tetta and the grandchildren followed. The next move was to Lausanne, Switzerland, while awaiting entry permits to England. They made it to London in December, 1938 and settled in. In September, 1940, the family was caught in the London Blitz while Hans was desperately negotiating passage out of the country. He succeeded, and they boarded a steamer in Liverpool, destination South America. The Almeda Star deposited them in Rio in October, only to be torpedoed and sent to the bottom on its next voyage. The following July they were on their way to America.

I met Marian's parents at their New York apartment. It was filled with art: Corot, Courbet, DeCamps, and classical music. Hans was dignified, proper, formal; Alice, elegant and warm. I asked Mr. Seidner if I could speak to him in private. He took me into the study and closed the door. I told him I loved Marian, wanted to marry her, and asked his approval. He fixed me intently and asked if I fully appreciated what I was doing. I assured him I did. He relaxed, grasped my hand, and announced to Alice that this young man wanted to marry Marian and there was nothing he could do to stop him.

With that settled, it was back to Boston, where Marian's tiny, book-filled apartment became a gathering spot for her Cambridge friends and my Boston political crowd. Marriage would wait. We were having too much fun.

CHAPTER 10

THE TOWN

Townies

My first encounter with Townies, as a group, was a football game at the Sullivan Square field in Charlestown one summer day in the late 40's. Winter basketball at the West End House was over and my team-mates on the Storrows were playing sandlot football after work against pick-up teams. The same conditioning that made the Storrows winners against bigger opponents on the basketball court was working in sandlot football. The Storrows were small, but fast. Shawnie Marshall, Frankie Fazzina, Ben Tankle, Sammy and Johnny Marinella, Dom DiFruscio, Sonny Grasso, were lugging fifty and one-hundred pound blocks of ice up four and five flights of tenement stairs every day in the Grasso family's oil and ice delivery business. I wasn't fast, but I had strong legs and determination. My assignment was to guard the passer at all costs.

One day the coach, the Marinella's older brother, Frankie, told us he had arranged a game for us with a team in Charlestown. He warned us to be prepared, for if we were to win the game we would lose the fight after the game; Townies did not like to lose to outsiders in front of their girlfriends.

The Townies weren't much bigger than us, but they were tough. I did my job, and the Storrows gained on pass plays, but the Townies were stronger on the ground. We were concerned because we held a small lead with only a few minutes left to play. In the huddle, the coach told us what to do if we ended up the winners — grab our gear and head immediately for the Sullivan Square el station. Fortunately for us, and for the Townies' pride, we lost.

Townies were not one hundred percent blood Irish because a lot of them had succumbed to the charms of Italian girls from the North End. But once accepted into the clan the wives were as fierce in their loyalty to the town as their husbands. There was no more formidable a pair in an argument than a Townie guy and his Italian wife.

IN HIS EAGERNESS to get the Boston urban renewal program moving rapidly Logue read the Townies wrong and overplayed his hand. He generated suspicion among politically savvy Townies when he appointed as project director an outsider from L.A. who sported a Harvard degree and an Irish name. His decision to negotiate the plan with the church hierarchy — Charlestown's three monsignors — split the community.

There was no dispute over *goals*. At the outset, Logue discarded a plan that would have demolished two-thirds of the housing stock for one promising 80% rehabilitation, new housing, and el removal. The opposition was to the *process*. Logue wanted the blessing of the clergy, who agreed to participate only if they were in control. This alienated the initially pro-renewal organization, Self Help Organization, Charlestown, (SHOC).

The confrontation took place at a public hearing Logue scheduled in January, 1963 to get approval for an early start on relocation housing. On the weekend before the hearing, SHOC's sound truck traveled the streets blaring the message "Save your home!" and distributed flyers depicting Logue and the monsignors on top of a pyramid symbolizing power fending off the public at the bottom. An angry crowd packed the Edwards School auditorium the night of the hearing and drowned out Logue and the monsignors with boos and catcalls. Prospects for an urban renewal project were buried.

The next morning I asked Logue's secretary, Janet Bowler, if I could see him. He was not the feisty Irishman of just a few days before. I told him that the project was not dead, but to be successful in Charlestown one had to go to the people, and I knew how to do it. Later in the day he called me in: "Frank, the mayor says O.K. I'm appointing you project director."

Overcoming Suspicion

I asked John McMorrow, the agency's administrative director, for help. I told him I wanted to move the Charlestown project staff out of City Hall and into the project area. To establish credibility we needed to be in the community; there was too much suspicion about what went on downtown behind closed doors.

McMorrow came through — we would get the entire ground floor of the Charlestown Public Library on Monument Square. I called a meeting to tell the staff about the move. I got some grumblings from the professionals, the city planners and architects, who preferred being close to downtown restaurants and shopping, but not from the political appointees assigned to the project.

Political appointees were spread among the various redevelopment agency project staffs, their salaries paid for with federal survey and planning grant funds. Three were on the Charlestown Project payroll: Arthur Guarino, Mike Matt, and Joe Charyna. My predecessor as project director had cut them out of the process, knowing they would report what was going on to McMorrow and he to the mayor. I *wanted* them to be in the process and to have this information go up the political chain. I told them that townies would not trust us unless we worked in the open, and if we failed, the mayor would be embarrassed and staff would have to be dismissed. I said they had to be involved in every aspect of project planning so they would know what they were talking about. They appreciated being included and went to work.

The Charlestown Public Library was a perfect location for our office. We set up shop in the large open room at ground level, with direct entrance from the sidewalk. We placed the drafting tables in the center, desks around the perimeter, and tacked street and plat maps to the walls. The most important map showed the building condition of each house. A survey of building conditions was required under the federal urban renewal planning rules. We color-coded each building yellow, orange, brown or black based on exterior surveys. Yellow or orange indicated no apparent structural defects. Brown was a danger sign. Black meant serious structural defects such as a sinking foundation and walls out of plumb — candidates for demolition. Staff let kids who wandered in sit at the drafting tables and use markers and colored crayons. Soon, students from the nearby Charlestown High School began coming in out of curiosity. Word spread quickly through the town about buildings that were marked black.

I knew we were in trouble when SHOC members James and Margaret Sweeney, and John Greatorix, marched in off the street, angrily demanding an explanation. When a Townie demands an explanation there is an implied threat of violence. The professionals froze. Mike Matt placated the delegation by explaining that the markings were tentative, based only on eyeballing from the street. He offered to have staff do an interior inspection and give owners a written report which they could go over with their own contractor. They said they'd be back.

The Sweeneys brought in the owners of buildings coded black, with surprising results. Rather than objecting, they were eager for us to inspect the properties and pointed out the problems they faced: leaky roofs, cold, porous walls with no insulation, inoperative plumbing, bad wiring, sloping floors, thresholds separated from the doors with cold air flowing in underneath. Joe Charyna, who had been Relocation Director for the West End project, got accommodations in the Charlestown Public Housing Project for several of these families who were living in uninhabitable conditions.

SHOC members Gene Hennessy and Danny Carr came in with an idea. Gene, a union guy, and Danny, owner of a gas station at City

Square, were concerned about the town's downward slide. They proposed that our staff give townies home improvement advice, not simply inspect for structural defects.

The city turned over to us a vacant tax-foreclosed house at 38 Cross Street. Everyone pitched in, gutting it, fixing up the interior, and painting the clapboards red. Our rehab chief, Charlie Dinezio, nailed up a sign "HOME IMPROVEMENT CENTER." The guys went all over town leaving flyers in barrooms and laundromats offering homeowners free home improvement advice. It worked. Townies began setting up appointments for home inspections. When the Kellys proudly attached large green letter "K's" to the window bays of their renovated three-decker we knew things were going our way.

Turf Battle

I got a call from Janet Bowler that Ed Logue wanted me to join him for a meeting with Port Authority Director Ed King. I hopped into my TR-4 and made it over the Charlestown Bridge into downtown in a flash.

King had been a star tackle at Boston College and went on to play pro football with the Baltimore Colts and Buffalo Bills. Though slightly overweight, he was still imposing. Superficially cordial, these two Irishmen were taking each other's measure. King controlled Port facilities, the Airport, the toll tunnel under Boston Harbor to East Boston, and the Mystic River toll bridge. He had designs on the redevelopment of the South Station terminal area. MassPort's bonding and eminent domain power gave King the upper hand whereas Logue was constrained politically and financially — dependent on the city council for project approvals and federal agencies for funding. Notwithstanding the imbalance, Logue projected power, whereas King was reserved, withdrawn.

King came bearing gifts — he had a plan that would rid the city of derelict cars abandoned on its streets. He explained how tow contractors would remove derelict vehicles from city streets, towing them to the Port Authority's Mystic River piers in Charlestown where a huge compactor machine would flatten them. The pancaked jalopies would be hoisted onto freighters for shipment to Japan as scrap. The press was making an issue of it and councilmen were under pressure to get abandoned cars out of neighborhoods, especially blighted Roxbury, where they were piling up. The city would benefit economically. Tow truck drivers and stevedores would get work. Boston city councilors would leap at the positive PR. King said that scrap giant Hugo Neu Proler would do for Boston what it had done for L.A. Logue said he would talk to the mayor about it.

After King left, Logue said he suspected there was more to this story than King was revealing, for he hadn't asked for something in return. This was uncharacteristic; King never gave anything away. I told Logue that John Neu was a law school classmate of mine, and if I remembered correctly, his family was in the scrap metal business. I would give him a call.

I reported back to Logue that the Neus owned the L.A. car compactor operation.

I offered to use my Naval Reservist weekend to fly a squadron Skyhawk to the West Coast for a look.

South Weymouth Naval Air Station Aerology charts showed a strong jet stream west to east across the middle of the country. To avoid those headwinds I planned a southerly route with three legs of roughly a thousand miles each, and a short final hop to Los Alamitos in L.A. The first leg was South Weymouth (NZW) to the Beaufort, South Carolina, Marine Corps Air Station (NBC), about eight hundred miles; next was a thousand mile leg to NAS Dallas (NBE), where I checked into the BOQ for the night. Early the next morning I was airborne to Yuma Marine Corps Air Station (NYL), about eleven hundred miles, where sand churned up by strong winds necessitated an instrument approach. After refueling, I was right back into the air for a short two-hundred mile final leg to the Los Alamitos Naval Air Station (NZJ). There, I rented a car to scope out the compacting operation in L.A. I was in for a surprise.

A few blocks from the scrap facility I got caught in traffic at a crawl. The cause of the jam was a procession of all manner of wrecked and burned-out cars in tow. Some were suspended front-end high behind tow trucks, others were attached to tow hitches, some were simply cinched with ropes lashed to the bumpers. They were bound for a facility surrounded by a tall concrete wall that prevented seeing into the site. At the entrance gate security personnel were directing the tow vehicles in, but when I attempted to follow they angrily waved me away.

I pulled in to the gas station across the street from the entrance and went inside. The owner acted as if he were expecting me and asked "State Environmental?" I didn't answer directly, but said I'd like to ask him some questions about the scrap operation. He thereupon unloaded on me: "Madonna mia! It explodes! See here — the calendar." The proprietor, with a heavy Italian accent, pointed to a large calendar on the wall, full of red "X's." Each "X," he explained, was a day on which there had been an explosion. He said that when they failed to purge the gas tanks the pressure exploded them. He pointed to the ceiling fluorescent light fixtures telling me that they kept breaking loose and he had to keep replacing them. I took 35mm slides of him pointing to red "X's" on each page of the monthly calendar. Then I shot a couple of rolls of film of the entrance gate with its ominous guards, the tops of the conveyor belt and cranes that were visible over the wall, and the procession of tow trucks and gypsy tow vehicles.

Mission accomplished I returned to Los Alamitos, changed into my flight gear, stowed my civvies, and checked Aerology for winds aloft. The jet stream was unusually strong from San Francisco due east across the country's midsection. I planned to take advantage by plotting a trip with three legs with my cargo of two rolls of 35mm film. The first would be four hundred miles up the coast to Alameda Naval Air Station on San Francisco Bay, (NGZ), refueling, then east in the jet stream for a long 1500 mile leg to NAS Olathe, Kansas, (NUU), and a final 1300 mile leg to NAS South Weymouth (NZW).

Night Flight

"A shoreless night, the pilot thought, leading to no anchorage (for every port was unattainable, it seemed), nor toward dawn. In an hour and twenty minutes the fuel would run out. Sooner or later he must blindly founder in the sea of darkness. Ah, if only he could have won through to daylight!

. . .

"What use to turn his eyes toward the east, home of the sun? Between them lay a gulf of night so deep that he could never clamber up again."

"Night Flight" Antoine de Saint Exupéry

Although I carried no Sidewinders, Sparrows, bombs or ammo when I left South Weymouth Naval Air Station on my mission, I was returning with a cargo of political dynamite: photographs documenting explosions from cars being compacted, and shots of derelict cars in tow jamming the L.A. streets around the scrap compound. When confronting the powerful it helps to have political ammunition, and I had it this time. Residents of Charlestown would erupt when they found out what Ed King had in store for them. I was eager to get back to Boston and expose the scheme.

I suited up, gave the A4B a pre-flight check, fired up the turbine, received Air Traffic Control Clearance for my first leg, and departed Los Alamitos in a dense brown smog blanketing L.A. I broke through the haze at 5,000 feet and was vectored to a northwesterly course skirting the California coast. The approach to Alameda Naval Air Station runway 13 was from the northwest, over Treasure Island in San Francisco Bay, clear of the crowded airspace around the Oakland and San Francisco airports to the south.

While the ground crew refueled the Skyhawk I grabbed a cup of coffee and a sandwich and checked Aerology for weather. Most of the U.S. was clear — *"CAVU"* — *ceiling and visibility unlimited.* A powerful jet stream arcing gradually northeastward from San Francisco, on the 38th parallel, to Boston, on the 42nd parallel, would propel me across the continent with only one refueling stop. I planned a 1500-mile leg to the Naval Air Station at Olathe, Kansas (NUU), followed by a 1300-mile leg to my destination at NAS South Weymouth (NZW).

Climbing to altitude, the western slopes of the Sierra Nevada Range ahead of me stood out, reddened by the sun on its way into the Pacific. Just over the mountains, white cumulus buildups darkened the terrain to the east. I leveled off at Flight Level 37, throttled back to 80% of thrust for optimum fuel economy, and activated the autopilot. Thirty seven thousand feet is roughly the demarcation between the troposphere below and the stratosphere above. At these altitudes turbojet efficiency is aided by cold air temperatures, and the thin air creates less drag on the airframe.

On autopilot I was able to devote my attention to the landscape and my maps. By comparing position with the airspeed indicator I calculated that the jet stream was giving me a one hundred knots boost. As I crossed the Wassuck Range bracketing California and Nevada I tried to identify the twin peaks: Montgomery on the California side, and Boundary Peak in Nevada, but cruising 25,000 feet over these prominences I couldn't distinguish one from another. Utah's Sevier Desert appeared as only a flat spot between the Wassuck's and the Colorado Rockies. The great peaks of the Colorado Rockies: Mt. Elbert, Mt. Lincoln, Gray's, were indistinguishable from my vantage point four miles above them. To a traveler weaving through the Continental Divide they were majestic, but I occupied a different universe.

The foothills of the Rockies tapered down into the Great Plains of Kansas, now inky dark. A hundred and fifty miles from Olathe, my refueling stop, I was cleared to descend at my discretion, and throttled back into a long, coasting glide. Even without navigational TACAN the glow over Topeka and Kansas City would have guided me to the field. When the tower didn't turn on the runway lights until I was in final approach I thought somebody must have been asleep at the switch. After landing I got the answer. I was the only jet aircraft at the field. Olathe was a multi-engine base, where pilots had plenty of time to line up with the runway centerline on final; so being a little late with the runway lights didn't make much of a difference as far as the crew manning the tower was concerned.

I filled out my flight log, got peanuts and candy bars from the vending machine, and watched the ground crew service the Skyhawk. When they finished refueling, instead of telling me the bird was ready to fly, the crew chief delivered bad news: the hydraulic fluid was low — too low to risk a flight covering the remaining half of the continent. Worse yet, they didn't have jet hydraulic fluid at the base. The closest location for hydraulic with the required specifications was the Air Force Base in Kansas City, thirty miles away. After assessing my worried expression for a few moments, the chief smiled, noted it was a quiet night, and offered to dispatch two sailors in a jeep to get hydraulic fluid. Divine Providence had intervened; it was destined that I fly through the night. I flaked out on the leather couch in Operations for forty winks.

"Lieutenant, lieutenant," I heard in my dream, and awoke to a sailor shaking my shoulder.

"You're ready to go" he said.

It was 2AM. I restoked on coffee, hit the head, strapped into the A4B, and while taxiing got clearance direct to my final destination, NAS South Weymouth, Mass.

I nursed the Skyhawk to its maximum altitude of 41,000 feet, then turned down the dimmers on the red instrument lights so the cockpit was as black as the void outside — an infinity of brilliant stars impossible to comprehend except when free of the troposphere. I was alone in the silent skies. Just to make sure I had actually been awakened from my forty winks and was not in a dream I radioed Air Route Traffic Control: "Chicago Center, this is Navy 4981, radio check, over."

"Roger, Navy 4981, this is Chicago Center, I read you loud and clear, over."

"Copy, Chicago Center, Navy 4981 out."

Except for the lights of Springfield and Ft. Wayne, the land beneath was dark. Lake Erie, to the left as I neared Cleveland, was a dull black. Unlike the sky, alive with stars, the earth was dormant, sleeping. About a hundred miles east of my home field destination a thin ribbon of red defined the horizon ahead, as the sun, well beneath the curvature of the earth, began establishing its power over the planet. I landed at the sleepy naval air station, my odyssey complete, wrapped my treasure: two rolls of 35mm film, in my red bandana, placed it into my ditty bag, revved up my TR-4 and sped into Boston.

I CALLED JANET Bowler from the photo shop and told her I had something to show to Logue.

I hooked up my slide projector, turned off the lights, and gave Logue a full performance, complete with an impersonation of the Italian gas station owner cursing the exploding compactor plant. Logue was excited. He told Bowler to set up a meeting with Ed King and have all the Irishmen in the office stand by to attend.

The next day a self-assured Ed King strode into Logue's office trailed by several members of his staff, all Sons of Erin. Logue was ready with his own Irish contingent: traffic engineer Bill McGrath, John McMorrow, Tom Deeley, attorney John Conley, and Townies Gene Hennessy and Danny Carr. After the handshakes and back-slapping, Logue introduced me as the Charlestown Project Director, explained that I was a Navy Reserve pilot and that I had just returned from a trip to L.A. to check out the car compacting operation. Everyone turned to me. I asked Janet to draw the blinds, turned on the slide projector and told the story. After the last slide Logue asked for the lights to be turned on and rose. Nobody said a word. King and his delegation were speechless. Members of our Irish gang fought to keep a straight face. The meeting was over. Janet Bowler courteously ushered King and his coterie to the elevator. We chuckled and everyone congratulated me. The future of the Charlestown project was now in my hands.

Ways and Means

"The coat of arms of the commonwealth shall consist of a blue shield with an Indian thereon, dressed in a shirt, leggings, and moccasins, holding in his right hand a bow, and in his left hand an arrow, point downward, all of gold; and, in the upper right-hand corner of the field a silver star of five points. The crest shall be, on a wreath of gold and blue, a right arm, bent at the elbow, clothed and ruffled, and grasping a broad-sword, all of gold. The motto 'Ense petit placidam sub libertate quietem' shall appear in gold on a blue ribbon."

Massachusetts General Laws, Part I, Title I, Chapter 2, Section 1.

Ed Logue assembled his project directors for an assignment. The state legislature had earmarked funds for a community college in Boston. Logue wanted the college to be sited in an urban renewal project area. He warned that if this became a battle between neighborhoods the city would lose this plum.

I called a staff meeting where there was a quick consensus that the old Charlestown State Prison site with the land around it was an obvious and compelling choice. Its location on a relocated Forest Hills/Sullivan Square elevated transit line meant the college would also serve Roxbury, the other major contender for the school — a perfect political solution. Staff attorney Fred Paulsen demurred, observing that the site was on tidal lands that the city didn't own, and an act of the state legislature would be necessary to convey rights to it. Everyone chimed in with encouragement: "Fred, you can do it!"

Fred was a young Harvard Law grad who, like John Bok, heeded the call of public service and left a promising career in private practice to join a talented cadre of planners and architects excited by the possibilities of the Boston Urban Renewal program under Ed Logue. We made a good team. I played my fighter pilot role — the bigger the challenge the better. Fred was the careful Boston establishment attorney, no less combative, but concealing it beneath a solemn, deliberative manner.

Accompanied by Fred, I asked for Logue's O.K. to pursue the Charlestown State Prison site. He wasn't optimistic: "The prospects are iffy. It is common knowledge that a grant of rights to tidal lands comes only when legislators are sufficiently induced to give away those rights. The city is in no position to do this, financially or legally. There would be too many complications if I or the mayor were to get involved. Nonetheless, give it a try, and good luck; you'll be on your own."

Fred thereupon locked himself in his office, emerging occasionally for a visit to the law library. Within twenty-four hours he produced the text of a bill conveying the land and a supporting legal analysis. John McMorrow agreed to get the bill filed by a state rep from Boston.

McMorrow succeeded in arranging for an expedited hearing of the bill before the House Ways and Means Committee. Fred and I arrived in the majestic committee chamber under the State House golden dome, laden with briefcases, display boards, an easel and a pointer. In a room full of lobbyists straight out of central casting we stood out — two serious young men in Brooks Brothers suits and conservative ties who were not glad-handing with the crowd. We were treated to a wondrous legislative performance.

Without a formal script, all the characters reprised roles they had played many times before. The clerk called up a bill, while the members of the committee, seated behind a magnificent oak dais, chatted among themselves, oblivious to the proceedings. The chairman recognized the sponsor of the bill, who introduced it, and perfunctory testimony was followed by a call for a vote, usually with no debate. Invariably, the vote would be unanimous one way or the other, patently foreordained.

When our bill was called Fred and I went to the front, set up an easel with maps showing the site and the boundary of the tidal lands, and waited. We were ignored by the members of the committee, busy talking among themselves, as well as by everyone in the hall. Eventually, the chairman, Representative Anthony Scibelli, noticing we were waiting to be recognized, beckoned me to the bench, leaned forward and asked: "Where is the Corporation Counsel? This is a Boston bill isn't it?"

I replied: "Yes sir. It is a Boston bill. I will be presenting it for the city, together with B.R.A. legal counsel Frederick Paulsen."

"And you are?"

"Frank Del Vecchio, Charlestown Project Director, Boston Redevelopment Authority."

"Where are you from, Frank?"

"I grew up in the West End. My family had to move because of the redevelopment project."

The chairman nodded, and after a few moments contemplation whispered to the chattering colleague on his right, then to the committee member on his left. As he did so, they stopped their conversations, looked up to discover Fred and me standing before the bench, and began passing the message down the line. Progressively the chatter stopped, ending with the last person at each end of the dais. As the members of the committee quieted, so did everyone else. For the first time that morning the room was in silence.

Chairman Scibelli then assumed a formal manner and announced to the attentive members of the committee: "Gentlemen. *Mr. Del Vecchio*, [enunciated slowly, with an Italian inflection — emphasis on the second syllable of the name], of Boston, will give a presentation of a bill which requires a grant of tidal land for the construction of a community college in Charlestown. Please proceed, Mr. Del Vecchio."

I explained how the community college at the old Charlestown State Prison site would be on a new rapid transit line that ran between Sullivan Square in Charlestown and Forest Hills in Roxbury, making it readily accessible to the poorest neighborhoods in Boston. I turned the pointer over to Fred, who outlined the boundaries of the historically tidal flats and explained the necessity for the legislation.

Chairman Scibelli: "Any questions?"

No answer. All the members were looking at the chairman quizzically.

"Hearing no objection, the clerk will mark the bill with a favorable report from this committee." House Ways and Means Chairman Anthony Scibelli brought down the gavel, and gave me a wink.

We had our bill!

A Hit to the Stomach

Townies had a personal relationship with the Kennedys. In Jack's 1946 campaign for Congress the entire family, including "Honey Fitz," the 83-year old former Boston mayor, climbed the stairs of Charlestown's three-deckers for tea with residents. They did the same in Teddy's 1962 Senate campaign. Every Seventeenth of June a Kennedy led the Bunker Hill Day parade through the Charlestown streets. Pastors at St. Catherine's, St. Mary's, and St. Francis DeSales campaigned for the Kennedys from the altars; the nuns did the same at the parochial schools.

Friday, November 22, 1963, was the darkest day in Charlestown history. I was surveying sites for new schools when news of the shooting in Dallas came in over the car radio. For days the churches stayed open, clergy at the doors, to a constant stream of residents, entire families in tow. Photos of JFK took the place of honor on Charlestown mantelpieces, bracketed by Pope John and Cardinal Cushing. The Town took a hit to the stomach that day and lost its swagger. In their common grief, the breach between residents and the clergy healed.

I settled into a work routine: building condition surveys, family and business relocation surveys, engineering replacements for ancient utilities— (some of the water lines were relics, wooden troughs covered by slate), negotiating locations for highway on and off ramps, selecting sites for new schools and a new high school and athletic field, completing and documenting the urban renewal plan, developing a budget, and preparing the application for a federal grant.

WEEKDAYS I WORKED all hours. Most weekends — when I wasn't on flight duty — I spent in New York, where Marian was helping a friend open up a small fashion shop on Fifth Avenue. Her tiny apartment, a half block from the Metropolitan, was a great location for exploring museums, art galleries, Greenwich Village restaurants, theaters.

In October, 1964, we were married in New York City Hall. The huge chamber was teeming with couples of every age and ethnicity, their babies and relatives. Best Man was my brother, Joe. Maid of Honor was Marian's sister, Susan. A functionary called out our names and escorted us to a small room adjacent to the chambers where an assistant city clerk with a stubble of beard stood at a podium shuffling papers. As we neared, the odor of alcohol on his breath sent Susan and Marian into paroxysms of giggles. When he pronounced us "Man and Wife by authority of the City of New York" Susan keeled over laughing. Joe snatched up the official documents as we dashed out of the building, destination the Russian Tea Room for drinks. At a reception in Susan's apartment that evening, her friend David Marantz, a jovial playwright, asked us where we were going for a honeymoon. When we realized we didn't have any plans, he said: "If you're going to do it, do it right. Go to Miami Beach, the Fontainebleau!" We did.

Back to Boston, where we rented a small Beacon Hill apartment at 81 Mount Vernon Street. It quickly became a gathering spot for Marian's circle and my political crowd.

The Second Battle of Bunker Hill

Back in the community, we took the urban renewal plan on the road, presenting our slide show *Your Home, Your Future, Your Charlestown* in every hall and clubhouse in town.

When SHOC diehards attempted a disruption they were shouted down by an audience angry about being interrupted as they viewed slides of familiar houses, streets, and their neighbors. Charlie Dinezio's home improvement crew had by this time assisted in dozens of home upgrades. Residents were impressed by new kitchens in interiors made airy with clerestory windows, and with renderings of new schools and fire stations, a new high school and athletic field, and sites for new housing. Conviction was building that our intentions were to improve Charlestown, not destroy it.

With the exception of El funding, all the pieces were in place for a public hearing on the plan. Gene Hennessy and Danny Carr cautioned us not to schedule a hearing until we had a guarantee.

The opportunity presented itself when Robert Weaver, the chief federal housing and urban renewal official, visiting Boston for a parade through the Roxbury urban renewal area, included Charlestown in his tour at the mayor's suggestion. I had a plan. I picked up Dr. and Mrs. Weaver at their Cambridge hotel in a rented convertible, top down, and headed for Charlestown over the Prison Point Bridge. From the bridge one could see the elevated structure over Main Street and the Thompson Square El station. I timed my speed to coincide with the approach of a train so that we arrived at Thompson Square just as the train entered the station above. I then proceeded underneath the elevated structure, the train screeching overhead as it twisted around the curves leading to the City Square El station. After a few minutes exposed to the banshee-like screams of metal wheels against metal tracks Dr. Weaver looked up and said: "That has got to go." Approval came after I submitted a lengthy technical report on the El's blighting impacts; federal bureaucrats needed justification that the $12 million expenditure was for substantive, not political reasons. With El funding secured, Logue scheduled a public hearing for Saturday, March 14, 1965, in the cavernous drill hall of the Charlestown Armory.

Notwithstanding our open planning process, a militant cadre of SHOC members was so distrustful of government that they equated all our efforts as merely part of a diabolical scheme to trick the people. They held secret organizational meetings to disrupt the public hearing with a "Second Battle of Bunker Hill." We learned through the Townie grapevine what they intended. They would line up speakers and keep the testimony going, for hours if necessary, until proponents tired and left the hall. When, by default, the majority of those who remained were antis, they would call for a vote. Forewarned, our mission was to turn out residents favoring the plan. Ed Logue campaigned using the Kennedy playbook, speaking to fraternal and religious associations and climbing three-deckers throughout the town for tea.

The day of the hearing Gene Hennessy, Danny Carr and their buddies pinned on *Erin go Bragh* buttons for the occasion and took front row seats. Nearly three-thousand residents filled the huge space. The first hour was given over to proponents, who testified that the city had met their demands and come through with everything that had been promised. They highlighted a concession they had extracted to protect residents — a unique proviso in the urban renewal plan that a taking of any property not shown on the official taking map would require board and city council approval. The crowd was enthusiastic. Next up were the opponents, angry because they were outnumbered and the sentiment was running against them. When SHOC member John Greatorix, in a state of great agitation, seized the mike and roared "They can take the fifteen million dollars and shove it up their ass!" the hall erupted. Thereupon, redevelopment agency chairman Monsignor Lally rose from his seat, called for a show of hands, and after surveying the crowd proclaimed "The Ayes have it!" The infuriated opposition, declaring it wasn't over yet, vowed to continue the battle.

The pandemonium at the Second Battle of Bunker Hill made headlines. Boston's newspapers and TV stations kept up the drumbeat for the next encounter, a public hearing before the Boston City Council set for Monday, May 11.

THE CITY HALL location at 45 School Street had been initially the site of the old Boston Public Latin School. In 1748, it was replaced with a city hall designed by Charles Bulfinch. The building stood until 1865, when the current granite edifice in French Empire style was erected. Our public hearing would be held in the city council chambers that James Michael Curley had dominated for half a century.

As a youngster walking the city with my father I was fascinated by the stories he told me about Boston's role in the American Revolution. Our route through Boston's narrow streets usually took us by City Hall on our way to the Boston Massacre site in front of the Old State House a block away.

SHOC was preparing for a revolution of its own. This time they were ready. On the day of the hearing they got to City Hall early. I spotted several of their stalwarts concealing paper bags containing tomatoes. The steep benches in the gallery, arrayed in a U over the main floor of City Council chambers, would be perfect launching spots for these missiles. When the doors opened they raced upstairs and commandeered every seat.

City Council President John J. Tierney looked out at a packed room ringed with TV cameras and banged the gavel to quiet the crowd. Logue sat at a table facing the nine council members. I was at his right-hand, my well-worn leather law school briefcase containing notebooks crammed with data on the floor beside me. Project attorney Fred Paulsen sat behind us.

After hurrying through the formalities, Tierney turned to councilor William J. Foley, Jr., an attorney, to start the questioning. Foley forthwith branded Logue as an outsider who butted into people's lives dictating what they could do with their property. Freddie Langone, playing to the gallery and the TV cameras, condemned Logue as a carpetbagger who comes into a city and destroys neighborhoods. Councilor Katherine Craven, lifting her substantial frame from her seat and pointing a finger at Logue, screamed he should be run out of town. Mayoral allies Christopher A. Iannella, John E. Kerrigan, George F. Foley, Jr., and Barry Hynes, waiting to see what kind of defense Logue would put up, raised only perfunctory questions.

Tierney recognized Foley for a second round of questioning.

The specificity of his questions showed that Foley had been carefully rehearsed by SHOC.

He challenged Logue to explain why such and such a house had been marked for demolition. I hastily jotted down the answer on a yellow pad I pushed in front of Logue: the particular property was structurally unsound and included in the new Edwards School site. Foley threw out another address and again I scribbled out the particulars. Working through a list of houses marked for clearance, Foley was intent on tripping up Logue.

After several minutes of this grilling Foley switched tactics, asking Logue to explain why a building adjacent to one to be cleared for a school *wasn't* being taken, since without it the site would be of irregular shape. Stalling for time, Logue danced around the question while I furiously scribbled prompts on the yellow pad: Our goal was to minimize demolition, and in order to avoid taking a house that could be saved we sometimes squeezed a school, park or housing site into an irregular boundary. I wrote: "Site meets School Department requirements without further enlargement; bridge off-ramp requires thirty feet lateral separation under highway standards." Etc., etc.

Foley continued rapid-firing questions, building up to an accusation: "Logue, you're perpetrating a sham! It will be impossible to save 80% of Charlestown's aged housing stock as claimed in the urban renewal plan because repairs will be of prohibitive cost; once the B.R.A. is in charge you'll have a free hand to tear down buildings." To drive this point home, Foley began peppering Logue, cross-examination style, with questions about construction costs based on type of property: clapboard, brick, shingles. Trying to keep pace with Foley I passed notes with cost data to Logue. Foley was just getting warmed up, while Logue was uncharacteristically tense, and sweating. The gallery was salivating at the show. The chairman was not about to intervene; the TV cameras were rolling.

Tierney mercifully brought down the gavel for a lunch recess. As Logue bent down reaching for his briefcase he whispered: "It's all yours, Frank, I'll be in Chilmark," and quickly exited. Fred Paulsen asked what he said. I told him the two of us would be facing the music alone because Logue was beating it to his summer home on Martha's Vineyard. Fred and I headed up School Street, past the Parker House, to Dini's Sea Grill, around the corner on Tremont Street, for Boston schrod and a draught of ale. Fred showed no emotion. My brain was racing.

When Tierney gaveled the afternoon session to order Logue wasn't at the table. Would the city council settle for the two young men in front of them? One could feel the tension and expectation in the room. What would the councilors do? If they broke up the meeting now they would lose this moment in the limelight. The question was answered when

Tierney nodded to Foley to resume. With a glance at the TV cameras, Foley picked up where he had left off. I feared the worst.

Foley tried to bollox me up with home renovation cost data that would prove his charge that rehab costs couldn't be financed. I was ready for him with details on Charlestown homes that had been fixed up with help from our staff, as well as information about various mixes of federally-guaranteed home improvement loans and housing rehab grants. I responded to each of Foley's questions at great length and in excruciating detail. Now it was Foley who was sweating. In exasperation he ended the interrogation, saying he would have more questions on the next round.

Each of the councilors in succession challenged me about the project. My preparation paid off; I was able to turn the questions around, building a compelling case for plan approval. After having faced questioning by professors Archibald Cox, Clark Byse, Benjamin Kaplan, Charlie Haar and their cohorts at Harvard Law School, the Boston City Council was child's play.

When it came to legal issues, Fred Paulsen, at my side, proved to be no relief for the frustrated members of the council. When one of them voiced skepticism about the feasibility of the community college site, Fred gave a legal dissertation on ancient rights to tidal lands under the Massachusetts Bay Colony Charter, and how state legislation had cleared the way for a conveyance to the college. The hapless councilors realized they would be unable to break the confident young attorneys in front of them, but as long as the cameras were rolling and every Boston TV channel was leading off the evening news with the goings on at city hall, they pressed doggedly ahead.

The hearings continued this way for six days, when they came to an end in a telling moment. An insistent councilor, persisting in his charge that more residents would suffer displacement by the project than we admitted, ominously asked me how *I* would feel if I had to be relocated. That gave me a dramatic opening. I answered: "Councilor, I know what it means to lose one's home. I grew up in the West End, and my family was among the twelve-thousand residents uprooted by its redevelopment. I vowed then to do everything in my power to ensure that would never happen again. It will not happen in Charlestown." This silenced the council. Sensing that a turning point had been reached, Councilor George F. Foley rose to "call the question," a motion that would end debate and trigger a vote for or against the plan. An infuriated Katherine Craven, objecting to an end of the proceedings, stood and spit out at Foley: "Sit down you bald-headed son of a bitch!" to cheers from the gallery. In the confusion, Tierney called a quick vote, which passed seven to two in favor of project approval.

The Second Battle of Bunker Hill was over. State and federal approvals followed quickly and the Charlestown Urban Renewal Project was underway.

CHAPTER 11

THE INNER CITY

I got a call from Pete Riemer, with whom I had worked at the Boston Redevelopment Authority. He was now deputy director of the Washington, D.C. redevelopment agency.

"Frank," he said, "we'd like to talk to you about being project director for the L'Enfant Plaza Urban Renewal Project. The project is bogged down in financial problems and lawsuits and we need someone with legal and redevelopment experience to tackle it. Ed Logue gave his O.K. to recruit you. Could you come for a look?"

"Sure," I said, "Good timing. Charlestown is moving along. My job in Boston is done."

The L'Enfant Plaza project was located south of the National Mall, part of a larger redevelopment area in the Southwest section of the District of Columbia. Residents and small businesses had been displaced to make way for a complex of commercial and government buildings. This kind of project was familiar territory for me. Like the West End, residents had been uprooted and stores shuttered, though on a much smaller scale. The plan, by architect I. M. Pei, was in the same genre of architectural brutalism as Boston's sterile Columbia Point Housing Project. I was eager to learn how the development game was played in D.C.

I asked my VAJ-911 squadron C.O. about my flying an A4B into the Washington, D.C. area. Anacostia Naval Air Station was no longer an option since it had been closed to everything except helicopter traffic. He doubted I would be able to park a Navy reserve aircraft overnight at crowded Andrews Air Force Base. I realized my hot cat pilot days were over. I flew commercial.

THE REDEVELOPMENT AGENCY was located in a downtown office building. As I was searching the directory in the lobby I heard: "Whose office are you looking for?"

"The D.C. Redevelopment Land Agency."

"I'll go up with you. I work there."

In the elevator my companion introduced himself as Reverend Douglas Moore and asked if he could be of help. I told him I was interviewing about a possible job on the L'Enfant Plaza Urban Renewal Project and was early for my appointment. I said his name rang a bell and asked if he had written a thesis at Boston University about churches relocating when their congregations moved.

Surprised: "Yes, I did."

I said I had come across his thesis when I was doing research for a law school paper about displacement from urban renewal projects. Moore asked if I had time for a cup of coffee.

In the lobby coffee shop I told Moore that I had been impressed by his ideas about the responsibilities of churches in poor neighborhoods. He argued that when a Protestant congregation shrinks as neighborhood demographics change to poor, the church should stay and minister to the newcomers irrespective of their religious affiliation.

I told him about the Boston Baptist Convention, which kept its church open even after immigrant Jews and Italian Catholics became a majority in the West End and how Rev. Mario Cestaro converted the chapel into a basketball court for neighborhood kids.

Moore was anxious to hear more — about law school and what brought me to Washington. I told him about the land grab that displaced the viable immigrant community I grew up in, how I resigned as a Navy pilot in order to go to law school and learn how the power structure operates. I told him about redevelopment politics in Boston, and about the Charlestown Project, designed to save the community, not obliterate it.

Moore said: "Forget L'Enfant Plaza. We need you for the Shaw project. Come with me. I want to show you the area. I'll call the receptionist and tell her you've been delayed."

We got into Moore's battered VW Beetle and headed uptown towards Logan Circle and U Street. As he drove, Moore told me about his work with Rev. Martin Luther King, Jr.

Moore met Reverend King when they were studying at Boston University Divinity School. They shared a belief in the mission of the black church to advocate for social justice.

Moore described King's failed attempt to plant his movement in the urban ghettoes of the North. In his Chicago Campaign, King had tried to create an organizational base of tenants' unions in the slums. It had not progressed as he had hoped. He was unable to mobilize residents around the problems of dilapidated housing and discriminatory housing practices. His efforts were stymied by powerlessness and poverty, and by the Daley machine's clever political maneuvering. King needed a more powerful strategy. That's where the Shaw project came in.

Using the federal urban renewal program as an organizing vehicle for the urban ghettoes was the brainchild of King's Washington SCLC head, Reverend Walter Fauntroy, and prominent Black D.C. attorneys Marjorie and Belford Lawson. The strategy was to exploit governmental eminent domain power and federal funding by *combining* city planning and community organizing. Instead of using these powers to *clear* slum areas they would be used to revitalize those areas *"with, by, and for the people"* who lived in them. What distinguished urban renewal from all other organizing strategies was the ability to gain control of *land*. Blacks historically couldn't and didn't own land. Ownership of land had a mystical quality to it. If this succeeded in Washington, D.C., King and the Southern Christian Leadership Conference would take the model nationwide.

Moore told me that the Washington, D.C. power structure had signed on, principally because banks had become nervous about mortgage loans they made for speculative land assemblies at the edge of the Shaw area. Developers were now setting their sights across the Potomac to Arlington, Virginia, and north to Bethesda, Maryland instead of the District. Banks needed to recoup their investments.

I thought this could be a winning formula. Banks would be able to cash out failed investments through federally-subsidized land takings. Collapsing property values in urban slums could produce a *coalition* between the power structure and residents, as long as residents believed they would benefit under the plans. If this could be demonstrated in Shaw it could be expanded to black slums around the country, where land had lost its value for private redevelopment. If slum dwellers could be organized to advocate urban redevelopment, that would be a powerful argument for politicians to turn the planning over to them. All interests would benefit, not only the landowners and banks, but residents as well. It came down to money and community organizing. The money had to come from Washington. It would not flow unless King and his lieutenants could organize the communities.

Driving through Shaw was depressing: second-hand stores, soul food restaurants, empty storefronts, trash-filled vacant lots. The Kennedy Playground at 7th and P streets, once a showcase, was covered with broken glass. Young black men congregated on street corners and on the steps of decrepit apartment buildings.

The interior streets presented a different, more encouraging picture: lined with rows of tidy brick houses, most of them well-maintained, many with vegetable gardens. I asked Moore: "Is that it? Have we seen the extent of the slums?" He said, "Don't be fooled by the row houses. Things are getting worse rapidly. We won desegregation, but now whites are moving out of the District and middle class blacks are leaving the inner city for better homes with more land in less densely populated sections of Washington. Left behind is a greater concentration of poor people. The poverty program can't keep up with the problems. We have to change the dynamics of this cycle. We need the money and the power to clear dilapidated slumlord housing, assemble sites for housing and playgrounds, and start a home rehabilitation program. Replacing the dilapidated Shaw Junior High School — "Shameful Shaw" — will be the rallying cry.

I told Moore the area had the ingredients needed to reverse its decline. The housing stock was of good quality. The area was only blocks from the White House and downtown and was well served by hospitals and colleges, including nearby Howard University. Readily accessible D.C. transit bus routes served scores of federal buildings and office buildings with thousands of jobs. I was enthusiastic about the prospects for the project.

My assessment animated Moore. He pulled over to a telephone booth at the curb, made a call, and returned to say Walter Fauntroy was at his church and would like to talk to me.

Reverend Fauntroy's New Bethel Baptist Church was in the heart of the area, in the 1700 block of 9th Street. We exchanged stories, hitting it off right away. We were the same age, and similar in purpose and motivation. He grew up in Shaw, earned a Doctor of Divinity degree at Yale, and returned to be the pastor of his neighborhood church. As a young divinity student he formed a bond with Reverend King and joined the Southern Christian Leadership Conference, where he coordinated the 1963 March on Washington and the 1965 Selma to Montgomery Voting Rights March. Notwithstanding the successes of the civil rights movement, he was distressed that the black populations of the urban ghettoes continued in a downward spiral of poverty, dependency, and powerlessness.

The idea of a new initiative for urban regeneration germinated when Fauntroy sought political assistance in acquiring a vacant parcel of city-owned land near his church to develop as low and moderate-income housing. Accompanied by attorneys Marjorie and Belford Lawson, he met with Walter Washington, Director of the D.C. Public Housing Agency. The conversation moved beyond the site in question to the possibility of a much larger undertaking with federal backing.

The federal urban renewal program could be the means to acquire slum land with federal funds, not just for public housing, but for redevelopment on a scale that could transform a neighborhood. To do so would require local governing body approval of a comprehensive plan of renewal. The discussions expanded to include District commissioners and members of the House District Committee, who agreed that the District should move ahead with the preparation of an urban renewal plan for the entire 675-acre Shaw district — from 15th Street on the west to North Capitol on the east — and its population of 50,000. Fauntroy used his appointment by President Lyndon Johnson as vice-chairman of the White House Conference on Civil Rights as leverage. He floated among White House staff the idea of an inner-city planning and organizational model that could channel the anger in the nation's urban ghettoes.

Fauntroy and the Lawsons sold the strategy to Dr. King and formed the "Model Inner-City Community Organization" (MICCO), as the organizing vehicle for planning the Shaw project. Robert Weaver, who had been appointed by Lyndon Johnson as the first Secretary of the newly created U.S. Department of Housing & Urban Development, expedited planning funds to the District of Columbia Redevelopment Land Agency (RLA), the official entity for renewal planning.

Fauntroy told me that what worried him now was staffing the project. Politicians were under great pressure to favor supporters with these federally-funded jobs. Every player in the D.C. Poverty Program had a candidate for the job of Shaw project director, but none had any experience. I agreed that at this critical moment it was essential for the project director to be a professional, not a political appointee.

Fauntroy asked me if I was interested. I said, absolutely, this was a job I could do. I told him my goal would be to train staff, and when the community was ready for it, turn over responsibility. Fauntroy said O.K., but for tactical reasons he would have to stay in the background. I would have to make the fight on my own.

D.C. Politics

"So, you stood me up for a ride with Doug Moore," Tom Appleby wisecracked as I entered his office late in the day, after my excursion through Shaw. "What do you think about the project?"

Tom Appleby was the executive director of the District of Columbia Redevelopment Land Agency. He owed his position to an appointed board, not to an elected mayor or city council. This was the case for all boards, commissions, and authorities of the District government, including the district commissioners. Residents didn't have the vote. The real power in the District resided in the House District Committee, which had split up responsibilities so that no one was accountable. The government of the District of Columbia was a bureaucratic morass.

I told Appleby I didn't know how the Shaw project, with all its challenges, could succeed, when the relatively straightforward L'Enfant Plaza project was at an impasse. In the absence of a strong mayor, who was going to knock heads together when bureaucrats couldn't agree? In Boston, Ed Logue had insisted on state legislation giving him planning as well as redevelopment authority. In Washington, the National Capital Planning Commission was an empire unto itself. How could the redevelopment agency plan an urban renewal project when it had no planning or zoning power? The situation was further complicated because there was no organizational coherence in the black community. A parcel of federally-assisted anti-poverty agencies were competing with each other. Each had its hooks into a pot of money to pay salaries. It was in their interests that power remain fragmented.

An even more fundamental problem challenged the project. Community renewal could not succeed unless residents were confident that investment in their homes would not be lost as their neighbors fled. The increase in slumlord apartment buildings and crime in the streets dimmed these prospects. The Poverty Program wasn't making a dent.

I told Appleby I had not spelled this out to Moore or Fauntroy because they had so much riding on the project. Moreover, I said, I had been so taken with their commitment I told them I thought it was a job I could do and that I was ready to sign on as project director.

Appleby said that although he agreed with my assessment, it was overly pessimistic. He told me President Johnson was going to appoint Housing Agency Director Walter Washington as mayor-commissioner, with strengthened executive powers. Walter Fauntroy was the best-known and most popular figure in the local black community, and had a bond with Walter Washington. As soon as Washington was appointed the redevelopment agency would approve a community consulting contract with Fauntroy's Model Inner-City Community Organization. Reverend Martin Luther King, Jr. would organize solidarity among civil rights organizations and the competing local anti-poverty agencies. The National Capital Planning Commission would understand these political realities and fall in line. His Redevelopment Land Agency as the conduit for Federal urban renewal funding had the means and flexibility needed for the task.

Excited by these prospects, I said, "Great news. How about the job of Shaw project director?"

Appleby balked, saying: "They wouldn't go for it."

I said: "Does that mean you wouldn't accept me because I'm not black?"

Appleby: "No. Not me."

"Who then?"

"Them."

"Them, who?"

"Well, the Urban League, the United Planning Organization, People's Involvement Corporation, Community Action Program, Black United Front, Shaw PAC, lots of organizations."

"Are you speaking for them?"

"No."

"So what makes you so sure?"

"C'mon, Frank. You know how it is."

"No, I don't know how it is. Call them up. Bring them in. I'll talk to them. I want to hear it from them."

"Frank, I can't do that."

"Yes you can. If you can't do it today, set it up for me. I'll come back and make my case with each of them. What's to lose?

"O.K., Frank. I'll do it. I'll arrange for you to meet all the players."

I called Marian and told her that I was making a pitch to be project director for a black inner-city area in the District and that I would be making a return trip to meet with local black leaders. She told me to go for it. My wheels were spinning on the flight back to Boston.

The Washington Post

Potomac

Sunday, April 9, 1967

Cardozo: "How We Gonna Help Each Other . . .?"

Banned in Washington

An article, by *Washington Post* Reporter Nicholas Von Hoffman, appeared on the Shaw Urban Renewal Project directed by Frank Del Vecchio. Von Hoffman also interviewed the Reverend Walter Fauntroy, MLK's lieutenant in Washington D.C., a colleague in the initiative to begin a model urban renewal project in D.C. that the SCLC might take nationwide.

Auditions

I was met at National Airport by a large gentleman in a black suit holding up a card: "FRANK." A limo and driver waited at the curb. In spite of busy traffic, the interior was quiet as a tomb. The last time I had been chauffeured in such style was in my grandmother's funeral cortege through the streets of the North End.

We pulled up at the R.N. Horton Funeral Home, 1322 U Street, where my greeter led me upstairs and motioned me to wait. After a minute he came out of the office and nodded for me to go in. Inside, several men seated at a table scrutinized me intently. The imposing figure at the center introduced himself as R.N. Horton, proprietor of the funeral home and chairman of the Black Businessmen's Association. These were men of few words; it was up to me to get the ball rolling.

I told my story — how I went to law school because my childhood neighborhood had been taken in a land grab and I wanted to learn how the power structure worked; how I learned that in addition to inheritance or purchase now there was a new way to get control of land: urban renewal. The federal government would pay a local government to take blighted land by eminent domain for redevelopment. This required designating an area slum and blighted, preparing a neighborhood plan, and obtaining political approval. The blighted Shaw area would qualify, but required an organization to do the planning and generate community support. With urban renewal, groups like their association, and nonprofit corporations formed by churches, could redevelop land for federally-assisted below-market-rate housing. Vacant sites could be paved as municipal parking lots. Land could be assembled to build a new Shaw Junior High School to replace the "Shameful Shaw" firetrap. Property owners could obtain home improvement loans. I told them about my experience directing a large urban renewal project in Boston and that I could do the same in the District, but had been told that as a white I would have to sell myself to the community. Theirs was the first group with whom I was meeting.

Mr. Horton thanked me and asked me to wait outside.

Thirty minutes later I was escorted back into the room, whereupon Mr. Horton rose from his chair and extended his hand: "We're with *you*, Del Vecchio!"

My next hurdle was a meeting with Sterling Tucker, executive director of the Washington Urban League. It did not start off well. Tucker was formal and cool. He spent most of the time telling me about his organization's work, which was building a base of cooperation between black leadership and the white business community. He gave examples of successes from this partnership, such as flight attendant training for young black women.

Tucker believed that even though blacks had won desegregation and voting rights, economic advancement would be tougher; there were no short cuts. Education, job training, a stable home environment and peer group pressure were essential elements. This demanded responsible community leadership, not self-appointed spokesmen paid by poverty program agencies. Those programs, he said, were being exploited by enterprising blacks for personal gain. Although he had the greatest respect for Reverend King, he was skeptical about Fauntroy's plans to organize the black community around urban renewal planning. He feared that opportunists would take advantage. Nonetheless, he said he had checked me out with friends in Boston, and wouldn't oppose my appointment; I was preferable to a local candidate without experience.

Tucker and his fellow black leaders were operating in a volatile arena with conflicting interests and aspirations. While cooperating on the core issues of racial justice, they were in a competition about ways and means and organizational survival. Except for the N.A.A.C.P., which stood apart from political confrontation, relying on the judicial system for breakthroughs, every other organization had its own leadership and constituency: CORE, SNCC, Urban League, Poverty Program organizations, SCLC. Martin Luther King's strategy was political accommodation through a white/black coalition. Firebrands like Stokely Carmichael frightened the established black leadership with "black power" slogans that threatened to sever bi-racial political coalitions.

I talked about these issues with my next interviewer, James G. Banks, executive director of the United Planning Organization, the local poverty program umbrella agency.

"Frank, I know about you. Walter Fauntroy briefed me.

"We have a problem in the black community. We won school, housing, public accommodations and voting rights, but our neighborhoods are in a downward spiral of poverty and crime.

"With an enormous expenditure of political coin, President Johnson got Congress to approve the Economic Opportunity Act. In the District alone, I am responsible for an annual budget of $15 million in education, job training, and neighborhood development programs delivered by a dozen organizations.

"We are failing. Sterling Tucker is right. We are fragmented. We rely on street workers who are clever and glib, but lack the know-how. Our training sessions are worthless.

"King and Fauntroy are counting on a coalition of organizations, churches, and leaders to take control of their own destiny by learning how to govern. The training ground is to be planning and carrying out an urban renewal project, which requires learning the structure of government. An approved urban renewal plan becomes the legal framework for land use in the project area. If we can create an organization in Shaw to do this it will be a model the president can use in black slums nationwide. This is our best chance to salvage the War on Poverty and demonstrate that the Great Society is not a waste of money.

"I understand the risks. What you experienced with the land grab of your Boston neighborhood could happen here. Not only do whites exploit blacks, blacks will do the same if given the power. We need to understand and control the uses of power.

"This is where you come in. I am supporting you as Shaw Project Director and have passed that information along to the UPO agency heads."

I was very moved by James Banks. I told him I would give it my all.

My last meeting was with Walter Washington, executive director of the National Capital Housing Authority. He wasted no time: "Frank,

I've talked to Tom Appleby, Walter Fauntroy, Sterling Tucker and James Banks. They believe you are the most qualified candidate for the job of Shaw project director. I've invited all the candidates to my office tomorrow for a meeting. You know what the stakes are. It will be up to you to make your case. Without acceptance by your competition, there will be problems."

I called Marian from my hotel room to fill her in. She said she never doubted I would be able to convince the people I talked to. She had one piece of advice for the next day: "Don't talk too much."

The conference room was packed. Everybody knew each other. I was the new face in town. I shook hands with as many as I could. Walter Washington entered, and took charge. He said there were a dozen candidates for the job of Shaw project director, all of whom were familiar to the people in the room, with the exception of Frank Del Vecchio. He would give me an opportunity to introduce myself and explain why I believed I should be appointed.

I said: "Gentlemen, I am a white from Boston. I will never be a political threat to any of you. I know the law of urban redevelopment and I directed a large, controversial project that won funding and is underway. None of you has that experience. If I am appointed project director my goal will be to train professionals like you how to do urban redevelopment, and then I will leave. I estimate it will take two years to develop the plan and get legal and funding approvals and another couple of years to assemble land, relocate displaced residents and businesses, and assist non-profit organizations to sponsor housing. I will be totally open and I will do everything in my power to assist you in taking a meaningful role."

Walter Washington asked for questions. There weren't any. The meeting was over.

Back in Boston, a day later, I got a call from Appleby:

"Frank. Congratulations. You're cleared. I'm preparing a press release. When can you start?"

"Right away. No need to delay. Marian's brother is with the State Department in D.C. and lives in Georgetown. We'll have a place to stay while we're looking for an apartment."

"Reverend Del Vecchio"

The Washington Post published a brief announcement of my appointment as Shaw Project Director, along with my picture bracketed by photos of "Assistant Project Directors" Reverend Douglas E. Moore and Reverend Arnor S. Davis. Appleby called us to his office as soon as I arrived to say that he was arranging for project offices at the agency. I reacted immediately: "We can't do that. We have to be in the community." Reverend Davis excused himself and in a few minutes returned to announce that the pastor of Shiloh Baptist Church, at 9th and P Streets, would let us use a building it owned at the rear of the church which it used for storage and occasionally as shelter for needy families. Fortunately for us it was currently empty. A surprised Appleby thanked Reverend Davis, wished us well, and remarked he hoped the three of us wouldn't forget about him. We squeezed into Moore's Beetle and headed out to our 9th and P Street headquarters.

Reverends Moore and Davis were contrasts. Moore was philosophically a civil rights militant, burning inside but keeping his emotions concealed for tactical reasons. Reverend Davis was old-school deferential. Moore had immediately related to me and considered me an important ally in the movement. Davis was worried about Moore's militancy and didn't know what to make of me. Moore circulated among agitators, Davis with the church establishment.

We approached the three-story row house behind the church. There were bars on the front door and on the basement and ground floor windows. We got a shock when we entered. Unknown to the pastor, a family was living upstairs. They came and went via a rear fire escape. Moore told them we'd make do with the ground floor and the basement. We piled the junk on the sidewalk for garbage pickup, bought cleaning supplies, and mopped floors and scrubbed windows until well after dark. The church custodian offered us some old wooden desks and file cabinets, folding tables and chairs. The next day we were joined by June Silver and Priscilla Deloach, who had been assigned to the project.

While we were setting up the office, a group of curious neighborhood kids walked in through the open front door. When Reverend Davis began to shoo them away I said "Let them come in. It shouldn't be a secret who we are and what we're doing." Reverend Davis let them pass, shaking his head disapprovingly.

I called a staff meeting and gave a speech. "Each of us is going to take part in every aspect of project planning. We're going to do this together. Our doors will be open and we'll go into the community to explain ourselves every step of the way. We will begin with family interviews in the neighborhood adjacent to the Shaw Junior High School. As you know better than me, the community wants it replaced with a new school. That will require taking property and relocating families. We have to know who will be displaced so we can prepare a relocation plan to meet their needs. There is going to be a major problem relocating large families since there are very few three or four bedroom units in public housing projects. The displacement of large, poor families is the major hurdle confronting the urban renewal program. We have to obtain reliable family data in order to justify an increased public housing allocation to the District.

"Tomorrow," I said, "Reverend Moore, Reverend Davis, and I, will begin knocking on doors and interviewing residents. I would like June and Priscilla to assemble base maps of the streets and census data by blocks so we can compare what we find to what's in the records.

The next morning, Reverends Moore and Davis showed up in their best Sunday suits. Armed with clipboards and family survey sheets we walked two blocks north of P to "Shameful Shaw," and climbed the stone steps of the first house we came to across from the school. Reverend Davis rang the bell and waited. No one answered. He rang again. No answer. I was ready to move on but he said: "Wait, there are people inside. I can hear them shuffling around." Doug Moore whispered to me:

"Frank. Residents will not open their doors. If they see guys in suits it is a collection agency, or the city; usually bad news." Arnor Davis rang again, and peered through the curtained window in the door with his hands shading his eyes. Then, the door opened, and a very big, very menacing black man stood in the entrance, arms crossed, surveying the three of us. Sensing we were not welcome, I was prepared to move along to the next house, but Reverend Davis removed his hat, and in his most pastoral manner said: "Brother, I am Reverend Arnor Davis, Assistant Pastor, New Bethel Baptist Church," and turning to Doug Moore, "and this is Reverend Moore," then, motioning in my direction, "and this is Reverend Del Vecchio." The tension was relieved. The imposing man in the doorway called inside: "It's O.K. It's three Reverends," and ushered us into the living room.

His wife offered us tea, which Reverend Davis accepted graciously. Reverend Davis asked her what church the family attended, and how things were going. As the three of us sat on the couch, curious children gathered, watching us deadpan. I decided this was the moment for me to perform my astonishing tea saucer trick. Instead of returning the teacup to the saucer, I put the cup on the table, and picked up the saucer with both hands, clutching it between the fingers, on the top, and my thumbs, on the bottom. I had concealed a quarter in my right hand, and as I picked up the plate held it between my right thumb and forefinger, hidden behind the plate. I slowly placed the edge of the saucer between my teeth, holding the quarter in a tension between the thumb and forefinger, against the back of the plate. All conversation in the room stopped. I was the focus of all eyes. I gave a little, reassuring wink to Arnor Davis, who was petrified. Now, the trick. By pulling the right forefinger back, the pressure of my thumb snaps the quarter loudly against the back of the plate, identical to the sound that would be made if I had bitten off the edge of the plate. I opened my eyes wide in feigned surprise as everyone looked wonderingly to his right and left, fearing the worst. Then I slowly removed the saucer from between my teeth, revealing it to be undamaged. The plate was intact. Reverend Davis winced disapprovingly. Doug Moore chuckled. The host burst into laughter and the children screamed with delight. The ice had definitely been broken.

Reverends Moore and Davis learned everything about the family, which I dutifully entered on the survey form. Word about the three Reverends quickly spread through the neighborhood, and residents happily opened their doors to us. A very clear demographic picture began to emerge. There were many more people living in Shaw than the Census had counted or that planners had estimated.

Adding up the Numbers

Priscilla Deloach and June Silver asked for a staff meeting. They had arrived at the troubling conclusion that building a new Shaw Junior High School, a lynchpin for neighborhood renewal, would be infeasible. Residents of apartments ringing the school site and needed for site expansion were primarily low income with large families. The District's inventory of multi-bedroom public housing units was not sufficient for relocation needs.

The analysis utilized the family composition data obtained by us three "Reverends." June and Priscilla entered the data onto IBM punch cards and extrapolated the information to the universe of apartments in the area from District property records. When they compared the results with U.S. Census block data, it was clear that the Census had greatly understated the population and significantly undercounted the number of children and occupancy by room.

Doug Moore frowned: "I expected as much. Census workers always undercount blacks!"

Arnor Davis differed. "Frank," he lectured me, "People are afraid. They are afraid that if an official finds out a family is overcrowding an apartment, the landlord will be cited and they will be evicted. They keep their mouths shut."

I said, "June and Priscilla have done a great service. This is critical information. At this point we can't let it get out, but we cannot solve this on our own. We have to pass this on to Reverend Fauntroy. The implications go further than taking property for a new Shaw Junior High School site. Site assembly and building clearance would not be an option in Shaw urban renewal planning."

Fauntroy said he knew housing was overcrowded, but hadn't realized the extent. He agreed that for the time being we should not make the survey results public within the agency. He would talk to Housing Agency Director Walter Washington about the need to lobby for an increase in the allocation of federal public housing units to the District, and the need to find sites for low-density family housing.

In the course of their research, Priscilla and June uncovered a pattern: the same names were cropping up over and over again as owners of apartment buildings with overcrowded units. I asked them to inventory real estate tax records for Shaw. The results precipitated another staff meeting.

"We've identified the Big 15!" they announced, "fifteen slumlords who own multiple properties in the District, concentrated in black areas. Many are in Shaw. Their buildings in Shaw are uniformly overcrowded, in deplorable condition, and grossly under-assessed compared to similar apartment buildings in the area. This is surely a pattern District-wide."

Doug Moore: "I knew it! There are sweetheart deals and kickbacks between slumlords and assessors in the District tax department. They are colluding to oppress poor blacks, who are afraid to complain. We can't keep quiet about this!"

Arnor Davis: "Brother Moore, you are right. Our people are being ripped off, and our own people in the government are a party to it. But now is not the time. We don't have the power. We have to move cautiously."

Fauntroy was distressed when we presented him with this information. He now realized the task was more challenging than simply organizing and planning Shaw renewal. The District Government had to be cleaned up. He asked us to write up our conclusions and provide him the documentation, but not to circulate it.

Because we didn't have confidence in the operation of the District Government, especially in functions related to redevelopment planning, we communicated less with our agency. Priscilla and June became a little paranoid, fearing reprisals if our evidence of illegal tax deals with slumlords came out. Doug Moore was itching for a fight, but Arnor Davis and Reverend Fauntroy counseled that the time was not now. A strange relationship with our agency heads emerged. They began to regard the Shaw project staff with suspicion.

Our work had to be packaged for submission to the Federal urban renewal administration as part of the survey and planning stage, but we did so innocuously. June and Priscilla transposed the IBM punch card data on family composition onto spread sheets, which we submitted to the planners together with the cards, without flagging the damaging conclusions. They did the same with property ownership data. The information was there for anyone to see, but it would require digging, which was unlikely.

It was more important now than ever for Fauntroy to take the lead in project planning, given these hazards. He set about recruiting staff for his fledgling organization, the Model Inner City Community Organization (MICCO). He had to reach beyond local professionals, most of whom were connected to the established power structure. I recruited two former colleagues at the Boston Redevelopment Authority: architect Tunney Lee, and Reginald Griffith, a talented young black planner, whom MICCO promptly employed as consultants.

Research and planning now proceeded on two parallel tracks: the agencies of the District government would go through the motions; Fauntroy and the Southern Christian Leadership Conference would tackle the nitty-gritty.

Black Power

"What do they call you, boy?"
"They call me Mister Tibbs!"

[*In the Heat of the Night* (1967), Dir. by Norman Jewison; United Artists]

A thrill rippled through the packed Republic Theater when Sidney Poitier gave his defiant answer to racist Southern police chief Rod Steiger in "In the Heat of the Night." In a later scene, when Poitier responded to a slap to his face by a white patrician plantation owner by returning the slap, the audience erupted.

Marian and I were seated in the balcony of the Republic Theater at 1333 U Street in Shaw, for a preview showing of the film. We lived a few blocks west, in the mixed Adams-Morgan neighborhood. The Republic and the Lincoln movie houses were more convenient for us than downtown. We felt comfortable in the black community, which was typical Southern courtesy. This evening, there was a marked change in the atmosphere.

The next day I talked to Arnor, Doug and Priscilla about our experience. Priscilla was fascinated by the possibility that the community might be at a turning point. She had debated black power with Stokely Carmichael when they were students at Howard, arguing that militancy would not work because Southern blacks were conditioned to accept their status. As recently as August, at a "Free D. C. Movement" rally, Carmichael got no support when he said that blacks had the "power to burn down this city" if their demands weren't met. King's moral coalition of whites and blacks under the banner of "nonviolence" was an essential political tactic. Yet in the movie theater, when a black struck back, the audience was delighted. She worried that King's strategy might be too late.

Fauntroy agreed that the slow pace of the District bureaucracy threatened his plans. He arranged for Dr. King to lead a parade through Shaw and deliver a speech, followed by a meeting in the White House.

Fauntroy asked me if I could help build support by expediting the process of qualifying area churches as non-profit housing sponsors. I arranged training sessions with the local FHA office.

The kickoff session was hosted by Reverend Ernest Gibson at his church. Marian joined me in a room filled with black clergy, with the exception of Father Gino Baroni, a crusading priest whom the Catholic bishop had appointed as a roving ambassador of goodwill to the black community.

I surveyed a room full of impassive faces and decided I needed an icebreaker to warm them up:

"Saint Peter stood at the Pearly Gates, scrutinizing each soul seeking entrance. Those waiting in the long line in front of him realized that they would be sent to the other place if he didn't admit them."

"Saint Peter beckoned the first person toward him, and asked his name."

"O'Toole."

"And where are you from, O'Toole?"

"Ireland."

"Saint Peter, after a pause, said to O'Toole:

"Spell *Dublin*."

"O'Toole did this with ease. Saint Peter waved him through the gates."

"The next person in line, when asked his name, answered 'Giovanni'."

"Saint Peter: And where are you from, Giovanni?"

"Italy."

"Saint Peter: Spell '*Genoa*'."

"Which Giovanni did with ease, and was waved into Heaven."

"Next in line was a black man, named 'Thomas'."

"Saint Peter: And where are *you* from, Thomas?"

"I'm from North Carolina."

"Saint Peter: Spell '*Czechoslovakia*'."

Nobody laughed. I was not off to an auspicious start.

Gridlock

Dr. King addressed a large crowd at Cardozo High School stadium on Saturday, March 18, 1967, and the next day led a parade through Shaw. I gave the official welcome on behalf of the District government.

In spite of the press the visit generated, project planning was bogged down. The National Capital Planning Commission was objecting to an expanded Shaw Junior High School site encroaching on the street pattern laid out by Pierre L'Enfant. Legal documentation was crawling through the District Building. I asked Howard Moskof, general counsel for the Redevelopment Agency, if he had any influence on the process.

Moskof said, "Frank, can I speak to you lawyer to lawyer, off the record?"

"Sure."

"There is very little interest in the District government about the Shaw project. The only reason it is on the docket is King's influence on the president, who needs to keep the urban ghettoes under control while he deals with the Vietnam War.

"Under other circumstances this might be enough to move planning along, but D.C. is facing worse problems than crime and poverty in Shaw. Suburban shopping malls are draining customers away from downtown. Merchants and bankers are panicking and demanding a revitalization plan. Planners are in a quandary about freeway expansion and the proposed rail transit system. They are against highway expansion, but there isn't enough population density to support rapid transit lines. Neighborhood renewal is an afterthought. The Downtown Progress association has more clout than Fauntroy and his ministers.

"If there is ever going to be a Shaw project, you and Fauntroy are going to have to do it yourselves."

"I figured as much. Since nobody in power really cares about Shaw, that means they should welcome us doing the work. This isn't as grim as it sounds. All I ask is that the agency not impede us."

Moskof: "I'll talk to Appleby. You know he is committed to the project. Go for it."

Spring, 1967

I told Fauntroy that no progress on the Shaw plan was being made within the District government and that we would have to do it on our own. If he would prepare the land use plan I would write the legal justification, the zoning changes, and the federal submission documentation. I asked him if his friends in the White House could pave the way for HUD funding.

Fauntroy confided in me. A breach over the Vietnam War had developed between President Johnson and Reverend King, who had denounced the war in a February speech at the L.A. Coliseum. The Johnson administration had initially signed on for King's plan in an attempt to head off more riots like Watts, but now the agreement was unraveling. King's status with LBJ was tanking at the same rate as the president's credibility. King's upcoming speeches in Chicago and New York would probably sink prospects for federal funding.

Nonetheless, Fauntroy said, we had to press on. I should tackle the legal and documentary workload while he mobilized the clergy.

MARIAN AND I were near the end of a long screening process by the Pierce-Warwick Adoption Agency and were readying our apartment at 19th Street and Columbia Road for a new arrival. In our final interview, agency director Linda Burgess mentioned a problem she was working on: how to discourage teenage girls from dropping out of school to care for their newborns. Burgess's idea was to station a van at Shaw Junior High School, staffed by a nurse and equipped with bassinets. A teenager could drop off her baby, go to class, and leave as necessary to nurse the infant. She wondered how the community would react to this service.

My response: "Well, Mrs. Burgess. Why not ask them and find out?"

"I would very much like to. How would you suggest I do this?"

"Come with me. I'll introduce you to Reverend Walter Fauntroy, whose church is only a few blocks from the school."

Checking my watch: "Rev. Fauntroy should be there at this very moment. He has a meeting scheduled with ministers."

Mrs. Burgess grabbed her bag. We dropped off Marian on the way and headed for New Bethel Baptist Church. Reverend Fauntroy and the ministers were extremely gracious. They liked the idea and said they'd ask parishioners to volunteer.

On our ride back to the agency Burgess was very animated. She turned to me with a broad smile: "I am going to get you and Marian the *best* baby."

And she did — first, a baby boy, and later, a girl.

Murphy's Law

"What can go wrong will go wrong."

King's anti-war speeches in New York in April, 1967 were the last straw in his increasingly strained relationship with Lyndon Johnson. On April 4, King not only infuriated Johnson, but alienated civil rights pragmatists in a speech at Riverside Church where he declared "A time comes when silence is betrayal." The NAACP and the National Urban League rebuked King for merging the civil rights movement with the peace movement. Disregarding the widening split, on April 15 King led a protest march of 125,000 from Central Park to United Nations Plaza.

Polls showed that most Americans, including blacks, disapproved of King's anti-war stand. Ironically, militant Stokely Carmichael and pacifist King bonded on the issue, marching together while King's long-time allies distanced themselves.

The splintering of the civil rights coalition did not go unnoticed by bureaucrats. District government officials adjusted to the political winds by giving the Shaw project just enough attention to justify salaries. HUD officials simply approved funding requisitions. Nobody was rocking the boat.

The big question was whether, when all was said and done, Johnson would punish King and defund the Shaw project, or allow it to move ahead. Fauntroy was betting on the latter. It was one thing for Johnson to rage against King in the privacy of the White House; it would be another to backtrack on his Great Society initiatives, especially in a summer of escalating urban unrest.

In mid-July, black confrontations with police erupted in riots in Newark and Detroit. Johnson had to send in federal troops when seven thousand Michigan national guardsmen couldn't end the burning and looting in Detroit. Johnson increased federal spending on the cities and appointed Illinois Governor Kerner to head an investigating committee.

During the summer and fall Fauntroy's planners worked on a land use plan while our small project staff ground out the documentation needed for the grant application. Poverty program agencies that initially had regarded Fauntroy as competition now cooperated in a united front designed to keep the federal money coming.

In February, 1968, the Kerner Commission found that the root cause of black frustration and rioting was lack of economic opportunity. It warned that the "nation is moving toward two societies, one black, one white — separate and unequal." These conclusions gave no one any comfort. It was an implicit assessment that the Great Society had failed. Johnson's credibility, in both war and domestically, was at an end.

ON THURSDAY EVENING, April 4, 1968, TV programming was interrupted with news that Reverend Martin Luther King had been shot in Memphis and pronounced dead at 7PM. Regular network programming then resumed. In frustration, Marian and I tried to get more news on the D.C. radio stations. There wasn't any. After brief announcements, local radio stations continued with their standard fare.

The telephone rang. It was Reverend Moore. He was inconsolable:

"Frank, are you listening to the radio? They shot our leader."

"Yes. We are just getting music."

"Can you help? I can't reach the mayor. Can you get him the message that they have to broadcast something else? He should be on the air."

I got Appleby on the phone and passed on Reverend Moore's message: By not responding, the media and the mayor were compounding the tragedy. I reminded Appleby how everything stopped when Kennedy was assassinated. King required similar respect.

Shortly after, Appleby called back. He said the mayor had decided to follow Police Chief Layton's advice to be as calm as possible and not do anything that might stir things up. I told Appleby that was a mistake. I called Reverend Moore, who couldn't believe it. He said that he was going up to SNCC headquarters (Student Nonviolent Coordinating Committee) at 2208 14th Street, NW, on the edge of Shaw, and hung up.

STOKELY CARMICHAEL BURST into the SNCC office shouting "Follow me." He was going to shut down local merchants. He headed south on 14th Street, telling storeowners to close up. The growing crowd began smashing windows and taking merchandise. When Fauntroy appeared and attempted to break it up Carmichael, brandishing a gun, continued on his mission. Police were not on the scene. They had been instructed to "keep cool." It was not until hours after the looting began that police arrived. By then the mob was out of control.

From our windows that night we saw the city burning. Washington was in flames. Troops cordoned off the black areas; traffic, transit and all movement was stopped. The next morning the streets were empty except for roving groups of young black men. Kids in the neighborhood park opposite us were throwing rocks at apartment windows.

Doug Moore telephoned to tell me about a meeting Fauntroy had called at his church. The debate was about what to do next. Carmichael proclaimed that territory which had been gained by the gun should be kept by the gun. Fauntroy said that guns were not the answer. Since property titles were tucked away in bank vaults in Maryland, the only

The Washington Post, April 5, 1968.

way for black people to get control of the land would be for the government to do this legally. Urban renewal was the answer.

AFTER THE NATIONAL Guard restored order, Appleby called me in to his office.

"Frank. The mayor would like you to represent the District government in a meeting with property owners who were burned out in the riots. Will you do it?"

I said I would.

I faced a huge, strangely silent crowd in a Bethesda, Maryland, synagogue. Most of the stores in the riot corridors were owned by Jews, now afraid to venture back into the area. They had lost faith in the ability or willingness of the District government to protect them.

I told them that the commercial properties in the riot corridors were now virtually worthless, even those that hadn't been looted and burned, and that it would take years for confidence to be restored. My advice was to lobby the federal and District governments to rapidly approve urban renewal plans that would take title to their properties. Under the rules of eminent domain the taking agency would appraise the property and offer the owners fair market value. While a property owner negotiated on price he could accept a "pro tanto" offer of partial payment if he needed immediate cash.

The consensus in the hall was to take this advice. The result was a coalition of white property owners, primarily Jews, who had spent much of their lives doing business in the ghetto, and blacks, advocating rapid approval of urban renewal plans for the D.C. riot areas. We packaged the plans with lightning speed. They were rubber-stamped by the D.C. Council and approved by HUD in two days. Appraisals and title searches were ordered and the legal work of offers and property takings got underway.

These actions had no tangible effect on the riot areas. They were uninhabitable. Residents fled in droves. Plans for new schools and playgrounds were not pursued. Would there be enough population to use them? Black churches formed coalitions with white churches to establish non-profit housing corporations if ever there were to be redevelopment. Some enterprising blacks moved quickly to option apartment buildings from slumlords who were no longer collecting rent, since tenants could get away without paying. Fauntroy had won an urban renewal plan for an area with no chance of renewal.

The fate of the city was now in the hands of its black majority. Fauntroy was its most respected leader, but of a constituency in which the most vocal were self-appointed spokesmen seeking personal advantage.

I continued to push the paperwork necessary to get the federal money flowing and property owners paid, but the District's mushrooming urban renewal bureaucracy disgusted me. Now that the newly empowered locals were in charge, they had little incentive to master the processes of government. My mission was over.

A telephone call from Massachusetts Senator Ed Brooke rescued me. Brooke, the first black U.S. senator since Reconstruction, knew of my work in Shaw and nominated me to direct a new HUD Office of Community Planning & Development for the New England Region. I was to be in charge of federal grants and oversight of community development projects throughout the six New England states, including the same urban redevelopment agency that had destroyed my childhood West End neighborhood!

I thanked those who had welcomed me into their community and told them it was time for me to go. They now faced a problem similar to mine. Both our communities had been destroyed; mine from without, theirs from within.

My wife and I and our two kids piled into our station wagon, destination Boston, latitude 42° 21' north, longitude 71° 5' west. I had come full circle.

EPILOGUE

The developer of Boston's Charles River Park project made a fortune. Displaced West Enders never got over it. The area's new residents formed a community over time. Charlestown prospered. It took thirty years for Shaw to recover.

Appendix I

Land Grab: The Politics Of Urban Redevelopment In Boston 1950-1960

March 20, 2010

The Boston Globe

Academic out of his depth in portrayal of West End[1]

RE: "West End's old guard reaches out to instill passion for cause" (Metro, March 14)

Herbert Gans's comments about the West End neighborhood that was demolished in an urban redevelopment land grab in 1958 are way off the mark. Gans, an academic from Columbia University, rented a flat in the West End to do observational research, but by the time he got there the neighborhood had profoundly changed. Residents knew what was coming and had been progressively leaving during the four years before the wrecking balls.

Gans is out of his depth in asserting that the West End was not a neighborhood.

He fails entirely to understand the dynamic immigrant Jewish and Italian community that was in transition from the old world to the new when it was obliterated. He was not there to see it. The upwardly mobile bulk of the population had left.

His description of the West End as a place where immigrants stuck to their own kind depicted those who remained, not what the community had been. West Enders were a mix, unlike the ethnically homogeneous Italian North End and Irish South Boston.

The "anger" Gans mentioned is universal when the powerless are overwhelmed by the powerful, especially when the government they hope will protect them is an instrument of harm.

Frank Del Vecchio

Miami Beach

The writer was born and raised in the West End, where he lived for many years.

The Accidental Candidate: John B. Hynes

For a half-century, the Silver-Tongued Demagogue, James Michael Curley, secured his political base by blaming the rich for the woes of the poor Boston Irish. His rhetoric, charm and wit, and an entrenched patronage machine, sustained him dating from his first election in 1899 as one of twenty-two Ward councilors, through four victorious campaigns for mayor, as a state legislator, four terms in Congress, and as governor.

In June, 1947, while serving a fourth term as mayor, Curley suffered a comeuppance. He was convicted of mail fraud and sentenced to six to eighteen months in the Danbury Federal Penitentiary. The Massachusetts legislature filled the vacancy by elevating Boston's unassuming City Clerk, John B. Hynes, a safe bet, to the post of "acting mayor." After Curley had been in jail only five months, President Truman commuted the remainder of his sentence. At the end of his first day back in the mayor's chair Curley proclaimed that he had accomplished more in that one day than had been done the five previous months. An enraged Hynes vowed, "I'll bury him!," and summoned friends to his home to mount a challenge to Curley in the November, 1949 election.

Curley's half-century of populist success, favors he could call, and fears of retaliation if he was crossed, were formidable obstacles to a campaign by the little-known city clerk. However, word rapidly circulated about Curley's belittling the gentlemanly subordinate who had conducted himself responsibly while managing the city's business, and there was speculation around city hall that this might be the turning point. Boston's economy was deteriorating, but the seventy-three year old Curley was offering only the tired promise that he would "get things done."

Two years after World War II the situation in Boston was grim. The city was losing population to nearby suburbs and suffering plummeting tax receipts. Its large public welfare rolls and a huge patronage burden were bankrupting it. Boston had never recovered from the Great Depression; when the war ended, its shipyards closed and its textile, garment-making and leather industries shut down. Instead of confronting these problems, Curley sang the same old tune, alienating the city's business and financial leaders as he stirred up resentment against the wealthy. With the city's accounts running dry, and few prospects for change, his promises of favor and threats of retaliation lost credibility, not only in the city, but with the state legislature, sinking any chance for a financial lifeline.

Although at age fifty-five Hynes was not a young man, he was of a different generation than the seventy-three year old Curley. Curley had his cronies; Hynes had a "gang" of young supporters. A trio of them: Pappas, Dazzi, and Kelly, proposed that he should cultivate a new, younger electorate, in addition to those whom Curley had alienated. In Jerome Rappaport, an enterprising twenty-year old Harvard Law School student from New York, they found an organizer for this campaign.

Rappaport caught the eye of the Boston press when he founded the Harvard Law School Forum, formed a board consisting of students who had been in the military, and dedicated it to the memory of Joseph P. Kennedy, Jr., who had left the law school to become a Navy pilot and was killed on a bombing mission. For the Hynes campaign Rappaport organized "Students for Hynes," in the process promoting not only Hynes but himself with radio addresses, lectures, and a newspaper.

On the home front, while Curley was deriding him as "the little city clerk," Hynes was making progress convincing bankers and businessmen worried about the disappearance of downtown customers that the city needed a new approach. His promise of a reconstructed "New Boston" secured the business establishment's support. The Boston press, which it controlled, soon was editorializing against Curley's "one-man misrule."

Hynes edged out Curley in the 1949 election. He would have to move rapidly to deliver on his promise of a "New Boston" because a change in the city charter meant he had less than two years before a rematch.

Orchestrating Redevelopment

Hynes used the eight weeks between the November election and his January 2, 1950 inauguration to put in place an organizational and political framework to carry out his plans. He slated the enterprising Jerome Rappaport, now in possession of a law degree, to be his confidential secretary and act as liaison to a commission to reorganize city government, with a mission to have the planning board adopt a master plan for redevelopment. On the political side, the objective was electing a slate of city councilors who would vote the mayor's way. A charter change on the 1949 ballot, effective in 1951, abolished the twenty-two member city council elected by ward, and opened the race citywide for the election of an at large nine member city council. The change from district to an at large council would dilute the influence of ethnic strongholds over councilors and strengthen the hand of a mayor who controlled a council majority.

Even if Hynes were to succeed in consolidating power in his hands he would be unable to deliver on his pledge to "reconstruct a New Boston" without the financial resources to do so. The city was on the verge of bankruptcy, and state relief was an impossibility, but an avenue had opened up: federal grants for urban renewal under the 1949 Housing Act, and for the construction of public housing projects. Paradoxically, urban renewal funds were available only to *clear*, not to *renew* neighborhoods. Unfortunately for their inhabitants, the aging housing stock and narrow streets of the city's oldest residential enclaves qualified those areas for clearance grants, the land to be sold to the highest bidder; Hynes simply had to decide which areas to have his hand-picked planning board designate "slum, blighted, or decadent." Next, his redevelopment agency appointees would submit applications for clearance grants, and for public housing. Public housing would expedite redevelopment by answering the political question about where displaced residents were to go. The challenge was to elect city councilors who would back these projects.

Hynes was the lucky beneficiary of the resolution of a four-year congressional struggle over the nature of a federal urban stimulus following World War II. The competing interests were finally reconciled when President Truman signed the Housing Act of 1949 on July 15, authorizing funds for slum clearance and redevelopment. The social reformers, who had long agonized over the health and welfare of poor slum dwellers, lost the argument, failing to achieve enforcement of sanitary and building maintenance codes as a remedy for the neglect of congested tenement districts. Lining up in favor of redevelopment were the planning and architectural professions, anxious to clear the decks and start with a clean plate, congressmen from urban districts, and mayors eager to obtain federal funds that would be funneled to cities and put power directly into their hands. The holdouts had been the homebuilding industry, which opposed funding public housing agencies versus providing subsidies to developers, and congressmen from rural districts whose constituencies were hostile to slum dwellers, subsidized housing, and bailing out cities. Ultimately, President Truman, intent on delivering on his Fair Deal promise to aid the millions of American families "living in slums and firetraps," pressured opposition rural congressmen and gained the house majority necessary for passage.

In Hynes's Boston of 1950, decisions on neighborhood clearance were based primarily on politics, not planning. Under Massachusetts law, an area designated as "slum, blighted or decadent" could be taken by eminent domain. Most of old Boston could readily be qualified as "decadent" since the narrow streets and housing density per se satisfied the criteria of an obsolete street pattern, irregular lot sizes, closely packed buildings, substandard structures, vacant lots, mortgage foreclosures or other conditions discouraging private investment. The findings by the planning board were mere strokes of the pen on a map of the city; no "planning" studies were necessary. The strategic decisions were political calculations: Where to start? How much to go for? Where would opposition come from? What would be palatable to the city council?

The answer to the question about where to begin was easy: start with the West End. It was prime land for redevelopment, situated at the foot of Beacon Hill along the banks of the scenic Charles River, only a ten minute walk from downtown. It would be the easiest target because its multi-ethnic population did not have the concentrated political clout of the city's entrenched Irish and Italian neighborhoods.

Hynes's appointees to the planning board acted quickly to qualify the West End for clearance by designating it "slum, blighted and decadent." The redevelopment agency followed with an application for a federal clearance grant, as well as an application for a massive fifteen hundred unit public housing project on the city's Columbia Point dump site. The housing project would displace no one, give work to favored contractors, be a bonanza to politicians who could count on getting their quota of units, and give Hynes a ground-breaking showcase before the September, 1951 mayoral primary election.

More problematical was the politics of how and when to proceed with the other areas the planning board identified as "decadent" because of housing congestion, narrow streets, or abandonment by landlords: portions of the South End and Mattapan, the Italian North End and East Boston, Irish Charlestown and South Boston, black Roxbury, Chinatown, and the depressed Scollay Square mixed boarding house and commercial district. Plans to redevelop the decaying Atlantic Avenue Waterfront and a declining Market District, Downtown, and the South Station area depended on the route of a Central Artery that would cut through Boston's core. Projects such as the construction of a garage under Boston Common and the reclamation of abandoned railroad yards in Back Bay would have to be negotiated with the financial and business establishment.

Hynes's rhetoric and style may have been a contrast to Curley's, but he was a product of the same ingrained Boston political culture and employed the same operational practices. Decisions were made within a tightly controlled power circle, rubber-stamped by appointed boards meeting in tiny rooms out of sight of the public, with no debate and scant press attention . The press did cover the city's debating showcase — City Council Chambers, where councilors gave the best performances in town other than those at the Old Howard. The big decisions in the Council were also foreordained. Insiders invariably knew the outcomes, and marveled at how ingeniously councilors enacted their roles — masters of feigned outrage and moral indignation.

All these plans were dependent on the 1951 mayoral rematch, which Curley vowed he would win, and electing a majority of the nine city councilors. The latter assignment went to Rappaport, who launched the "New Boston Committee" to build a solid base of banking and business support for its slate. This time, Hynes did "bury" Curley, defeating him by a two-to one margin. The New Boston Committee slate won five of the nine city council seats, assuring Hynes of the majority necessary for his redevelopment agenda.

The Insider: Jerome L. Rappaport

The first tangible delivery on Hynes's pledge to build a "New Boston" was the monolithic 1500-unit Columbia Point public housing project rising on a forty-acre section of a putrid city dump site jutting into Dorchester Bay. Its towers could be seen from many vantage points, including three-deckers on the slopes of South Boston. The Boston Housing Authority, ignoring the recommendations of consulting architects to include commercial and community facilities in the project because that would mean delay, contracted with a politically connected firm for a solely residential development. The project's cookie-cutter layout consisted of fifteen identical seven-story structures and twelve identical three-story buildings, containing apartments with tiny rooms and thin walls, at a location with no stores, services, or public transportation. Its only neighbor was the adjacent garbage dump, the destination for the disposal of animal carcasses and food refuse from the city's market district, operating twenty-four hours a day.

At the April 29, 1954 ribbon-cutting ceremony, Mayor Hynes was flanked by Archbishop Richard J. Cushing, city councilors, state legislators, and political supporters, all congratulating each other on the achievement. Hynes proclaimed that with this project the city's housing shortage had ended. There was more to this announcement than met the eye. It meant that the city could now satisfy the federal requirement that relocation housing be available for residents displaced by redevelopment. It was a green light for the Housing Authority to enlarge the scope of clearance of the West End from the originally designated 37 acres to the entire 48-acre neighborhood and its 12,000 residents.

Expanding the project area posed a political problem for Hynes, for it would renege on assurances given some influential property owners that their buildings would be spared. The major landowners in the area, the Catholic Archdiocese and the Massachusetts General Hospital, had been taken care of. They had secured early commitments that their holdings would not be touched. The Archdiocese negotiated a deal ensuring not only that Saint Joseph's Roman Catholic Church and rectory would be spared, but that an acre and a half would be added, presumably for a new parochial school. Lawyers for the Massachusetts General Hospital saw to it that the project boundaries excluded blocks adjacent to the hospital, where it was using straw buyers to acquire property for expansion. The MGH also had its eye on the nearby Winchell School, which wouldn't be needed after the neighborhood was cleared.

When property owners who thought the project would bypass their properties learned of the project area's expansion, they took their complaints to Gabriel Piemonte, the city council's only Italo-American member. Piemonte, an up and coming young attorney from the North End, had been solicited by Rappaport to run under the "New Boston Committee" banner in the 1951 campaign. The first test of his loyalty had been the April, 1953 vote that got the West End project rolling. Piemonte voted to approve the submission of an application for a project planning grant. Luckily for him the vote was little noticed by his constituents. If

Piemonte were to fall off the bandwagon now, it could jeopardize Hynes in the upcoming mayoral election, where he was facing a challenge from John E. Powers, the powerful minority leader in the state senate. Powers was already charging Hynes with planning giveaways to commercial interests. Hynes could not afford a public breach affecting the Italo-American vote. Piemonte was not a sure thing, for he had recently split with the mayor over land takings in the North End and Chinatown for an elevated expressway through downtown. So, for the time being, Hynes left the West End project dormant.

The 1955 race was a repeat of Hynes's 1949 contest with Curley, but without the assistance of Rappaport, who had opened up a law practice a block from city hall specializing in tax abatements. Hynes won, but by only a ten percent margin — which was low given an incumbent's patronage power. Nonetheless, the decks were now cleared to move ahead with approvals for West End redevelopment. The project would be the showcase for long-delayed action by Hynes on his commitment to the business community to reconstruct a "New Boston."

Rappaport made his move. He formed a development corporation, Charles River Park, Inc., composed of Boston realtor Theodore Shoolman, developer Seon Pierre Bonan, and N. Rappaport & Son, his father's New York firm. Rappaport acted as General Counsel and spokesman. The Housing Authority took the next step. In mid-April, 1956, even before federal project approval and before any land takings, it invited sealed bids for purchase of the entire project area, still in private ownership with a population of twelve thousand. A public auction among the bidders was to follow the bid opening. At its Nov. 15, 1956 meeting, the Authority Board awarded the contract to Rappaport's firm at a price of $1,493,000 for 48 acres of cleared land, and waived the public auction. This was a blatant giveaway to Charles River Park. Its bid was 90% less than the $13.5 million estimated cost of the eminent domain land takings — an incredible write-down of land value. The Housing Authority had greased the process by obtaining a conveniently low appraisal of the value of the cleared land —about a dollar a square foot for commercial land and seventy-five cents per square foot for residential land. Mayor

Hynes crowed that the city was getting a bonanza because Rappaport's payment of $1.47 per square foot for commercial and $1.15 per square foot for residential was a 50% premium over the appraisal.

The deal was sealed when the Housing Authority, immediately after selecting Rappaport's firm, voted to waive the public auction among the bidders that was to have followed. The Authority contended that an auction was not necessary since the bid exceeded the city's appraisal; it claimed, moreover, that a higher sales price would force the developer to charge higher rents. (One of the selling points for the project was that it would provide middle-income housing.)

The obviously preordained action by the Housing Authority, and Hynes's defense of the award to Rappaport, did not sit well with two established Boston realty firms that had submitted bids: Max Kargman's First Realty, and Vernon Realty Construction represented by Martin Woolf. They took their complaints to city councilor Gabriel Piemonte. He called for the council to hold a public hearing.

The city council chamber was packed the evening of November 26, 1956. Members of the "Committee to Save the West End" were there to protest. They had been frustrated by the lack of coverage by the Boston newspapers, who served as cheerleaders for the clearance project. That evening would be no different. The press was interested only in the drama of challenges by the developers whom Rappaport had aced out.

Kargman and Woolf charged that dispensing with the auction violated the bid requirements. They exposed a major loophole in the contract: Charles River Park could avoid taxation by simply flipping ownership to a limited-dividend corporation it would form. Not a single member of the Housing Authority Board attended the hearing. Instead, they trotted out their front man, executive director Kane Simonian, to take the heat. When a frustrated Piemonte put him on the hot seat, Simonian counterattacked, threatening dire consequences if the council were to overturn the Housing Authority's action. The only outcome of the hearing was the realization that nothing was going to stand in the way of the sale of a cleared West End to Rappaport's Charles River Park.

As the inevitability of the project sank in, opposition fizzled out. Even the landlords who had sought Piemonte's help in saving their buildings shifted gears. Residents were abandoning the West End in droves, leaving rental apartments empty. The longer it took for the project to be approved and the land taken by eminent domain, the lower property values would be. Banks had long ago redlined the West End guaranteeing that no improvements would be made, when, in 1950, the Planning Board designated it a slum, blighted and decadent area.

If there had been any lingering question about the fate of the West End project it was answered a month after the council hearing, when Mayor Hynes appointed Rappaport the city's Assistant Corporation Counsel. All the machinery was now in place. The press and the establishment beat the drums to get the project moving. Protests and petitions were to no avail. The agency public hearing approving the project was pro forma. Italo-American politicians went through the obligatory motions of appealing the project, but the outcome was foreordained.

On January 24, 1958, the contract for federal grant funds was signed. The redevelopment agency followed on April 23 by filing a mass taking of all private property within the boundary of the 48-acre project, excepting Saint Joseph's Church and Rectory, and two historic sites, the Old West Church and the Harrison Gray Otis House. The residents who remained received eviction notices by registered mail, with instructions to pay rent to the clearance agency, advising they could submit a written claim for up to $100 in documented relocation expenses. Letters sent to the owners of 315 businesses in the area advised they could file a claim for moving expenses and direct property loss up to a max. of $2500. Those families who filed claims received relocation payments averaging $69; the businesses filing claims averaged $1405 payment each.

The last headline in this saga was anticlimactic. The mayor and redevelopment agency ignoring the city council's call for an investigation into charges that the winning bidder on a $937,000 demolition contract had been told to "bid low and then come back for extras," ordered demolition to proceed. This was understandable, for if "no extras" had been the standard for city contracts, the whole edifice of municipal contracting would have collapsed quicker than the buildings in the West End.

West Enders scattered. Small shopkeepers abandoned their stores. In a few months the area resembled the bombed-out cities of World War II, with a few stray dogs picking around the rubble. From time to time a resident, grieving for a lost home, returned as I had, looking for a familiar street corner. Soon, even the lampposts that held the last landmarks — the street signs — were gone.

Post Mortem on "The New Boston"

In 1959, announcing he would not seek another term as Boston mayor, John Hynes threw in the towel. He had lost the confidence of the business establishment, which had counted on him to reverse years of cronyism and incompetence in city hall and pull the city out of its decline. Although his ten-year tenure was scandal free, and he was considered by his peers to be the "dean" of mayors, he had failed in his mission.

Hynes never understood his failure. Right up to his farewell speech he clung to a vision of a new, reconstructed city rising out of the rubble of the old. He proved incapable of recognizing that the seeds of rejuvenation had been in his hands — the social and economic vitality of the city's neighborhoods and shopkeepers, and the pedestrian character of the city's core and waterfront. The projects for which he was responsible — the sterile Columbia Point public housing project and the clearance of the West End to make way for the Charles River Park development — were blunders. The first was on its way to social disintegration. The latter destroyed a functioning community that had the potential to renew itself from within.

Hynes was not alone in failure. Older urban centers nationwide were suffering middle-class flight to FHA-insured suburban subdivisions. Older downtowns were losing customers to suburban shopping malls with easy access and lots of parking. Planners, architects, bankers and businessmen, figuring that cities had to compete with the suburbs on the same terms: assemble in-town land for redevelopment, and provide parking, were accelerating their decline.

The redevelopment strategy proved elusive and infeasible. A vision that might have worked for the development of barren farmland on a city's outskirts proved destructive for the dense and historic City of Boston. Soon after the Planning Board in 1950 identified more than 2700 acres blighted or decadent and marked them for clearance, banks red-lined those areas, freezing out investment. The process fostered abandonment and disinvestment.

As residents and businesses became aware of this they began looking elsewhere. Over Hynes's tenure the city lost thirteen percent of its population. In 1959, Moody's lowered the city's bond rating to "junk" status. Now, the bankers who had put him in office were in a panic.

New Horse, Same Track: John F. Collins

The Boston Establishment thought they picked the right horse when they put their money on John B. Hynes for mayor, but he came up lame. His dream of a "New Boston" got buried like a time capsule in the rubble of the West End; commercial projects were not off the ground; the tax base continued shrinking while the patronage and welfare rolls stayed the same; real estate taxes were killing businesses as their customers were disappearing.

The establishment faced the unnerving prospect that candidate John E. Powers would be installed as Boston's fifty-second mayor. This long-term pol, now the powerful president of the State Senate, in his losing campaign against Hynes had echoed Curley's refrain that the city was selling out to the big boys while the little guys suffered. Although this time Powers had toned down his rhetoric, landowners feared his election would guarantee bankruptcy for the city.

Powers dominated the field for the September, 1959 primary. Political handicappers rated city councilor Gabe Piemonte second, State Rep. James Hennigan, Jr. third, and school committeeman John P. McMorrow bringing up the rear. The odds quickly changed when Hynes, in a seemingly off-hand remark to reporters, mused: "I wonder how John Collins would do against Johnny Powers?" and Collins immediately filed to run.

As a young attorney, a veteran, and a member of the State legislature, John F. Collins had supported Hynes in his successful 1948 race against Curley. He got attention as an anti-gambling, anti-bookies candidate in a 1954 losing bid for State Attorney General. The following year, while campaigning for a seat on the Boston City Council, he contracted a crippling case of polio, refused to drop out, and won. When his term ended he was appointed Suffolk County Register of Probate. Collins was giving up a lifelong sinecure in filing for the mayor's race.

The Collins candidacy posed a dilemma for the Boston business establishment. Hynes had been a reliable plodder in the heavy going of Boston politics, and they could count on Collins to continue on the same course. If they bet on Collins and he won, although they would be in the driver's seat, this would assure retaliation by Powers. Any doubts on their part were resolved when Collins came out aggressively for the passage of a state sales tax, their best hope for real estate tax relief. He had to be the choice.

Prominent members of the business and banking fraternity began meeting in secret to plan strategy. They held their meetings in a boardroom at the Boston Safe Deposit and Trust Company, near the vault. They decided to quietly funnel money to Collins while maintaining contact with Powers. When word of the secret meetings got out, the press christened the group "The Vault."

Collins surprised the handicappers by beating out Piemonte to take second place in the September primary, thereby making it into a November runoff with Powers. Powers had polled only a third of the total vote. Emboldened, the Vault filled Collins's campaign war chest and drummed up support at the Tavern Club. With this backing, Collins unloaded his guns on Powers, linking him to bookies in a campaign that called on voters to "Stop Power Politics."

Collins handily won the November runoff. At his January 4, 1960 swearing in he pledged to cut spending and cut taxes in an "Operation

Revival." Although expressing deep concerns about urban renewal, he announced he would continue the program under a broadly empowered administrator reporting directly to him. In Collins the Vault was getting a younger, more energetic, and more inventive mayor than Hynes, but one who would be running on the same track with the same treacherous footing.

Thunderclouds formed and quickly turned the political footing to mud when Collins's nemesis, John E. Powers, presiding over the state senate, scuttled Collins' property tax relief bill. Collins turned to public entrepreneur Ed Logue from New Haven to save the city. For the next seven years, with Boston as the big top and himself as impresario, Logue would produce "The Greatest Urban Renewal Show on Earth."

APPENDIX II: AIRCRAFT FLOWN

	North American T-6SNJ "Texan"	North American T-28 "Trojan"	Lockheed T-33/TV2 "Shooting Star"	Grumman F9F-2 "Panther"	Beechcraft SNB	Grumman F9F-8T "Cougar"	McDonnell F3H-2N "Demon"	Douglas A4B "Skyhawk"
Length (feet)	29'	33'	37' 9"	37' 5"	34' 2"	44' 4"	58' 11"	41' 4"
Wingspan (feet)	42'	40'	38' 10"	38'	47' 8"	34' 6"	35' 4" (25' 4" wings folded)	27' 6"
Height (feet)	11' 8"	12' 8"	11' 8"	11' 4"	9' 8"	12' 3"	14' 6"	15'
Wing area (sq. feet)	254	268	235	250	349	337	519	260
Empty weight (lbs.)	4,158	6,424	8,365	9,303	6,175	12,787	21,287	10,465
Fuel Capacity (gals.)	110	178	825	1,063	205	1,063 internal (+ 300 w/ext. tanks)	1,506 internal (+524 w/ext. tanks)	1800 (w/ three external tanks)
Loaded weight (lbs.)	5,617	8,500	12,071	14,235	7,500	16,698	31,145	24,500
Power plant	Pratt & Whitney R-1340 550 hp	Curtis Wright R-1820 1,425 hp	Allison J33-A-24 6,100 lb. thrust	Pratt & Whitney J42-P-6 5,950 lb. thrust	(two) Pratt & Whitney R-985 Radial 450 hp	Pratt & Whitney J-48-P-8-A 7,250 lb. thrust	Allison J71-A-2E 9,500 lb. thrust	Pratt & Whitney J-52-P-408 11,220 lb. thrust
Max. speed (m.p.h.)	208	395	600	575	225	630	716	674
Cruise speed (m.p.h.)	145	207	455	487	140	475	553	498
Range (mi.)	730	1,060	1, 025	1,353	1,200	600	1,180 (max. 1,320)	2,000 (with tanks)
Service ceiling (ft.)	21,500	39,000	48,000	44,600	26,000	43,000	42,650	40,600
Rate of climb (ft./min.)	1,200	4,000	4,870	5,140	1,850	4,800	14,350	8,440

Appendix III

My Flight Students

Principal Instructor		Check Ride Instructor	
Anderson	Littrell	Ackerman	Johnson
Beal	Lubberstedt	Adema	Kaempfer
Benson	Matus	Allertus	Kellams
Bradley	McGrath	Beck	Kerlin
Bradshaw	Meacham	Bird	Knight
Breitenhurt	Melvin	Britton	Kresl
Browning	Moberg	Buckley	Linnes
Buckley	Montgomery	Buile	Lund
Cambell	Mullen	Byington	Manly
Carr	Nagel	Cervind	Markley
Chambers	Odom	Chase	Meyer
Copeland	Ogle	Chelf	Mihalke
Culp	Pack	Clancy	Morgan
Davey	Pederson	Cole	Moss
Day	Peterson	Coyne	O'Neill
Dowell	Phillips	Cremp	Perrotta
Ellington	Quinn	Criley	Pettinati
Exley	Roberts	Danly	Powers
Farrell	Robinson	Doebbler	Purdy
Fleming	Rowland	Dorches	Reed
Gallegly	Ryan	Edwards	Scampini
Gibbon	Sanders	Elharis	Scharpen
Gleary	Sandler	Evans	Schoske

Principal Instructor		Check Ride Instructor	
Grub	Schneider	Farrand	Shaffert
Gutierrez	Shuler	Flinchum	Sherman
Hammond	Sileika	Galli	Smith
Hanson	Simpson	Ganz	Snow
Hellman	Sipple	Garvin	Somer
Hilton	Sterling	Golden	Stagg
Hoggett	Swingle	Gran	Stephens
Huggins	Temple	Hallas	Stirling
Hunter	Thompson	Hamilton	Trauber
Jackson	Tibbetts	Hatcher	Tunnel
Kagawa	Titsworth	Hite	Turnbull
Kizer	Todd	Horellou	Vaught
Kluemper	Trupp	Hotz	Walker
Knapp	Von Hendy	Housden	Wyckoff
Koga	Wilkie		
Kuhn	Wilson		
Lee	Winchester		
Legg	Wright		

LETTER TO ELIZA

January 9, 2009

Dear Eliza:

This is a picture of me with Reverend Dr. Martin Luther King, Jr., March 18, 1967 at the Cardozo High School stadium, Washington, D.C.

I was about to go the microphone to welcome Dr. King on behalf of the Washington, D.C. government. As you can see from the photograph, Dr. King has his speech in his hand.

Dr. King was ready to speak to the residents of this inner-city section of Washington on the need for them to become involved in improving their neighborhood. As the director of this improvement project, I was working with Dr. King and a group of local ministers, several of whom are in the picture, including Reverend Ernest Gibson, with the pipe, and behind him Reverend Channing Phillips, with the clerical collar. A crusading Catholic priest, Rev. Gino Baroni, is standing behind me.

A little earlier, while waiting for the crowd to gather, I observed how Dr. King prepared for the speech. On this chilly Saturday morning in Washington, he sat alone in the passenger seat of a car reading and re-reading his speech. I could see his lips moving soundlessly as he did so.

After the introduction, Dr. King stepped onto the stage, and placed his speech on the podium. He looked at the large crowd seated in the stands, and for a few moments simply scanned their faces. There was total silence. Dr. King looked down at his text, then up and began speaking, slowly and softly, then more forcefully. Not once did he read from his notes. He had committed the speech to memory and improvised as he delivered it, repeating phrases for emphasis.

The next day, Sunday, there was a parade through the Shaw project neighborhood, with Dr. King, his wife and his children riding in an open convertible. The crowds were large and enthusiastic. Planning for the project had gotten off to a good start. Tragically, a year later, on April 4, 1968, Dr. King was murdered in Memphis, Tennessee. The people whose spirits had been lifted by Dr. King's speeches and his determination became despondent, and the same Washington, D.C. streets along which the King family paraded in March, 1967 were torched by rioters and looters. It took thirty years for the neighborhood to recover.

Your grandfather,
Frank Del Vecchio

Made in the USA
Charleston, SC
08 January 2017